John M.D. Hunter

An Information Security Handbook

Springer

John M.D. Hunter, BA (Hons), FBCS, CEng
CISM Group, Cranfield University, RMCS, Shrivenham, Swindon SN6 8LA, UK

Series editor
Professor A.J. Sammes, BSc, MPhil, PhD, FBCS, CEng
CISM Group, Cranfield University, RMCS, Shrivenham, Swindon SN6 8LA, UK

ISBN 1-85233-180-1 Springer-Verlag London Berlin Heidelberg

British Library Cataloguing in Publication Data
Hunter, John M.D.
　An information security handbook. – (Computer
　communications and networks)
　1. Computer security
　I. Title
　005.8
　ISBN 1852331801

Library of Congress Cataloging-in-Publication Data
Hunter, John M.D., 1940-
　An information security handbook. / John M.D. Hunter.
　　p. cm.
　Includes bibliographical references and index.
　ISBN 1-85233-180-1 (alk. paper)
　　1. Computer security – Handbooks, manuals etc.　2. Computers – Access
control – Handbooks, manuals etc.　I. Title.
　QA76.9.A25 H87 2001
　005.8 – dc21
　　　　　　　　　　　　　　　　　　　　　　　　　00-066154

Typesetting: Electronic text files prepared by author
Printed and bound at the Athenæum Press Ltd., Gateshead, Tyne and Wear
34/3830-54321 Printed on acid-free paper SPIN 10882470

To Phillipa, Clare and Charlotte

Acknowledgements

I would like to thank all members of CISM Group at the Royal Military College of Science for their help, advice, general support and forebearance in connection with the preparation of this manuscript. Special thanks need to be given to Tony Sammes and Edna Day. Without them, this project would never have got off the ground. I would also like to acknowledge the helpful comments from the students of all the Design of Information MSc courses held at RMCS since 1990. Special thanks also need to go to the staff at Springer, London, for their truly professional assistance. Finally, a word of thanks must go to my family who have had to put up with the "grumpy lump" while this book has gone through its gestation.

Contents

Chapter 1

Introduction

1.1 Why a Book about Information Security?

This book began life as a simplified guide to the United Kingdom government security guidelines for the protection of information systems. This guide was used as a text for third year and post–graduate courses at the Royal Military College of Science where a large proportion of the students are either in the armed forces or in government service. Most of these guidelines are entirely appropriate for conventional commercial systems. Some of them are not and are specific to government systems and national security. It is hoped that the inappropriate bits have all been removed.

The aim of this book is to provide answers to five questions:

1. What is security?
2. What are the security problems particular to an IT system?
3. What can be done to reduce the security risks associated with such a system?
4. In a given situation, what are the appropriate security countermeasures?
5. How should one set about procuring an information system with security implications?

It is not the intention to provide a very detailed technical description of every IT security issue, but to introduce the reader to the spectrum of security problems which are to be found in such a system. Should you, the reader, need, or want, a more technical approach then you should consult some of the other books or papers listed in the Bibliography in Appendix H at the very end of this book. Where a reference seems to be particularly appropriate, there is a specific recommendation in the text.

It is fairly straightforward to create and maintain a system in the absence of any competition or opposition. However, in the real world, there is bound to be some competition and opposition. Security measures are those which

1

are taken to maintain the effectiveness of a system in the presence of either competition or opposition or both.

In the commercial world, competition is taken for granted, thus security ought to be equally accepted. In some lines of business, such as road building or field sports, there can be active opposition by pressure groups as well. In government business, particularly foreign affairs and defence, the main concern is that of opposition rather than competition.

You may well ask what is the difference between "competition" and "opposition"? Competition implies that the behaviour of all parties is governed by some rules even if they are only informal. Opposition implies that there are no rules. The only restrictions on agencies trying to interfere with the workings of the system in question are those imposed from economic restrictions.

What do we wish to achieve using information system security techniques? There could be any number of possible aims, but the four most likely are:

Availability: maintaining a specified level of service to the user.
Integrity: ensuring that the data in the system is corect and is not tampered with.
Confidentiality: ensuring that sensitive information does not leak from the system.
Exclusivity: denying to a competitor any possible benefits he may derive from any information that should come into his possession.

Of these, the one which most people associate with security is confidentiality. However, this may not be the most important. It is impossible to generalise across all information systems which particular security aim should be the most important. For example, in static intelligence information systems, confidentiality is likely to be given priority. However, in a commercial information system, availability could well be considered more important and a bank is likely to lend more effort to securing the integrity of the data. This book is not so much concerned with the choice of security aim but with the techniques available and the choice of techniques most suited to achieve that aim.

1.2 Some Conventions

In the subject areas of computer science and security there is a lot of jargon. Many of the words in these technical dialects of English are everyday English words which have been overloaded with new meanings. So as to minimise confusion, I have attempted to comply with a convention where words which are everyday English are printed in a normal (Roman) typeface, but words used as jargon are printed in a `teletype` typeface. To complicate the issue still further, some words, when used in an appropriate context, have a technical legal meaning. For example, the English word "confidential" is an adjective which, when applied to a piece of information, implies that the information is not for general circulation. In a security context, the word `confidential` can be applied to information, or an object bearing information, which has to be safeguarded in a particular way. The UK government, as a result of the many UK Official Secrets Acts, has defined the concept of legally binding rules as to the care and handling of `CONFIDENTIAL` information or artifacts carrying such information.

The `teletype` font is also used for computer commands and computer file names in the text. This is to distiguish commands and file names from jargon.

To supplement these conventions, an *italic* typeface is reserved for other technical terms or jargon. Finally, nearly all of these words should be defined and explained in a glossary, Appendix G.

1.3 Risks

The technical term for an attempt to interfere with the workings of a system is a *threat*. Associated with any threat is a likelihood that the threat might be put into practice. Also associated with a threat is the damage (or rather the cost of the damage) which would result from the threat being carried out. This combination of threat, associated costs and likelihood is known as the "risk". A paranoid individual is quite capable of dreaming up an alarming list of possible threats including the building being struck by a meteorite. However it would be impractical to take precautions against every possible threat. The concept of *risk* is very important as it provides a metric which allows threats to be prioritised.

It is convenient to categorise the threats to information systems into different types of threat:

Physical threats: for example, theft of equipment.

Personal threats: for example, employees being bribed to divulge commercially sensitive information.

Technical threats: for example, a software error causing valuable data to be corrupted and lost.

Before we can discuss any security measures, we need to list the possible threats to an information system. Among the possible threats are:

1. Access to the system by unauthorised personnel. Once access has been achieved they may be able to:

   a) tamper with the equipment so as to facilitate any of the threats listed below;

b) deny use of the system to *bona fide* users or significantly reduce the performance of the system;

c) introduce erroneous information into the system, thereby misleading the *bona fide* users (possibly for someone's individual benefit e.g., a payroll computer);

d) extract from the system information to which they are not entitled.

2. Coercion or persuasion of someone who is authorised to have access to the information system to carry out one or more of the above.

3. Vulnerabilityvulnerability of essential services to deliberate or accidental tampering:

a) the electrical supply (static or tactical);

b) air conditioning; and

c) water (or other coolant supplies) for super-computers.

4. Access to the communications associated with an information system with a view to:

a) extracting information from the system by monitoring the communications into and out of the system;

b) inserting bogus information into the system by spoofing another genuine system or user.

5. Deliberate modification of the computer hardware or software before it is delivered so as to enable an agent, at some later date, to sabotage the system.

Software that contains unauthorised features is a particular problem. There are a number of colloquial terms that have arisen concerning them:

A sleeper is a dormant program implanted during software development which can be activated to circumvent the users' security measures.

A Trojan Horse is an implanted program which performs (or seems to perform) some useful service for the user but which compromises the security of the system at the same time.

A virus is a covertly implanted program which is designed to replicate itself onto all discs and tapes on a given machine and, if possible, contaminate any other connected machine.

The threat posed by such software is that it is quite unexpected and it can affect an operational system before the presence of the threat can be detected.

1.4 Information Sensitivity

In any sensible discussion about information security there is a need to define a shorthand method of describing the sensitivity of information. In this context, the term sensitivity means the "costs" arising from the information getting into the wrong hands. However, rather than attempt to place a monetary value on information, it might be rather more useful to define information sensitivity categories, in a similar fashion to the UK government's *classifications* (UNCLASSIFIED, RESTRICTED, CONFIDENTIAL, SECRET and TOP SECRET). Having defined these categories, it is a relatively simple matter to assign information into one of these categories on the basis of the costs of the information leaking out.

In the commercial world, one way of categorising information would be as follows:

Unrestricted information is that which is intended for the general public, e.g., publicity and catalogues.

Private information is that which is of no direct concern of the general public. However, such information, when combined with certain circumstances, could cause some embarrassment. Items covered by this category are internal memoranda and the diaries of managers and senior executives. This category is analogous to the UK government RESTRICTED classification.

Confidential information relates to information which would give competitors some commercial advantage if they were to gain access to it before the owners of the information had been able to exploit such information. (The inference is that such information will cease to be CONFIDENTIAL at some time in the future.)

Secret information is commercially very sensitive information which is never likely to be disclosed in the normal run of events, e.g., a family secret recipe.

Obviously, no effort should be expended in the protection of Unrestricted information. Private information should be protected by sensible procedures; however, because of the difficulty of assigning a "cost" associated with the disclosure of such information, it would not seem reasonable to spend large sums of money to protect such information.

With Confidential and Secret information, it should be possible to assign a notional cost associated with its disclosure. Such information is normally protected by a combination of procedures and physical measures such as safes. In particular, the dissemination of such information is restricted to those people who can be trusted to honour the confidentiality of the information and have a need to know the information.

1.5 Information Importance

There is a second property of information which needs to be taken into account when formulating a security policy. That is, how important is it to ensure that the information is not destroyed or lost, either by accident or deliberately. This property of the information is its *importance*. As with information *sensitivity*, it is possible to define a number of categories of *importance*:

Inconsequential data is that which has little or no bearing on the business; it is not worth taking any specific measures to safeguard such information.

Significant data is which, if it were not available, could affect the efficiency of the business.

Essential data consist of the records which, if they were to be mislaid, would materially affect the efficiency of the business and could affect relationships with other organisations, suppliers or customers.

Vital data consist of the records without which the business could not function together with those records which the business is legally obliged to maintain.

Inconsequential data could range from information that has gone out of date to unsolicited sales material. Just because information is deemed to be inconsequential, it does not mean that it can be tossed into a waste-paper basket. It may still be sensitive and will need to be safeguarded even though it is no longer worth keeping.

Significant data would consist of the majority of internal memos, minutes and letters held in the filing system of the business and the diaries and appointment books of the more senior members of the organisation. The fact that copies of such records are usually kept on more than one file could be deemed sufficient safeguard for such information.

Essential data would include most correspondence with external organisations particularly correspondence of a contractual nature. Such is the importance of this data, it is necessary to formalise the safeguards for such data. In particular, there should be a designated "master copy" kept in a safe place where it cannot be tampered with.

Vital data could consist of financial records or classified document registers which an organisation is legally obliged to keep and maintain. The conditions under which all such records are kept will be determined partly by the relevant legislation. In particular, the records should be kept in conditions where any attempts to tamper with them or destroy them should be obvious.

1.6 Countermeasures

There are a number of possible countermeasures which can be deployed to defend the security of an information system. No single defence mechanism is sufficient in itself; all the defence mechanisms have to be used in concert to produce effective security. Of course, the proportion of effort spent on each mechanism will vary from system to system.

The defence mechanisms can be crudely classified under the following headings:

Physical security consists of the traditional methods of keeping unwanted people out of reach of the information system. This is the first line of defence in any security system; only if this is inappropriate, or fails, should the other defence mechanisms be called into use.

Personnel security consists of ensuring that those who are authorised to come into contact with the system are trustworthy, responsible and not vulnerable to pressures from unfriendly agencies. The people that these measures should cover include:

1. the users - those who derive a direct benefit from the system;
2. the operators - those who manage the system;
3. the engineers - those who install, upgrade and repair the system;
4. the programmers - those who write, upgrade and correct the computer software;
5. visitors - those to whom the managers and users wish to show off the system.

Radiation security consists of ensuring that any electronic emissions from the system or its communications do not contain information useful to a potential enemy.

Software security consists of arranging programs to perform checks before certain transactions are allowed. An example of this is a password dialogue before a user is allowed to interact with an information system. A second form of software check is to ascertain whether a user, having logged in correctly, is authorised to read or change particular items of information.

Procedural security consists of all the other measures which complement those measures listed above. Examples of procedural defence mechanisms are:

1. A login to the information system can only be achieved after convincing the information system that you are who you claim to be, for example by the use of a password.
2. Vital information held by the system is copied and held at a remote (secure) site to be used to repair the system should its information become corrupted for any reason.

1.7 Information Warfare

Threats to information systems have been reinforced by the concept of *information warfare*. Such is the reliance of modern society on information systems, it is postulated that one section of society can attack another throught their information systems. These conflicts could be waged between nation states or between rival commercial organisations (such as between British Airways and Virgin Atlantic) or by revolutionaries trying to overthrow a government.

An information warfare scenario is an example of outright "opposition" where there are no holds barred. Information warfare attacks would normally consist of any combination of two or more of the following:

- an attack on communication systems to gain intelligence;
- an attack on communications to plant erroneous or misleading data;
- an attack on communications so as to reduce their performance (effectiveness) or to effect a complete denial of service;
- hacking computer systems to gain intelligence, change data or deny service;
- distributing virus infected software mainly to effect reduction or total denial of service.

Attacks on another organisation's information systems with a view to reducing their effectiveness, or even completely destroying them, have become known as *information warfare*. Politically, conflicts waged using information warfare are very attractive for at least two reasons:

1. they tend to be non-lethal, in other words nobody gets killed or seriously hurt as a direct result of information warfare;
2. there is not much public sympathy for high technology systems and their implementors. When a high technology system crashes, the general public reaction tends to be along the lines of "Huh! I told you that it would never work!".

The London *Sunday Telegraph* of 7th February 1999 reported that a 14 year-old Israeli schoolboy concocted a software bomb which was attached to an e–mail to an Iraqi government Internet web site with the blandishment that the enclosure contained a virus capable of wiping out Israeli web sites. The Iraqi site administrator accepted the bait and invoked the batch file attached to the Israeli schoolboy's e–mail, which resulted in the Iraqi web site being rendered inoperative. The moral of this story is that if a mere schoolboy can mount a successful attack of this sort, system administrators had better be prepared for attacks mounted from agencies backed by far greater resources.

This book is not aimed at information software. However, most of the defences mentioned here would be usefully deployed in the defences against most information warfare attacks.

1.8 Management

One could be forgiven for thinking that information security consists of the indiscriminate application of the security techniques described in this book and other manuals. To underline this point, if one takes a less technical analogy, one would not use every meter and oscilloscope in a workshop when checking to see if a mains plug was correctly wired up to a kettle. The ideal situation is for an investigation to be conducted to determine the actual security threats and then to select and implement the appropriate countermeasures. The investigation and selection processes are essential parts of security. In fact these activities are part of the security management process.

An organisation which takes information security at all seriously should make a very senior official personally responsible for the management of all information security activity. The degree of seniority should be such that the official should report directly to the managing director (or local equivalent). This official should be responsible for drafting and implementing the security policy, which should be endorsed by the managing director.

The matter of what form a security policy should take is discussed in Appendix D.

Perhaps the most difficult aspect of managing security is the determination of the actual risk posed by a specific threat and the costs to the organisation should the threat actually materialise. When this information is available, it is a relatively straightforward matter to determine what countermeasures would be cost effective. In practice, accurate information as to the actual risks is almost impossible to obtain. Similarly, any costings will be only crude estimates. Consequently, scientific management of information security is far from easy to achieve. The practical approach is to follow the principles of good practice which hopefully are to be found in the body of this book.

Finally, it must be stated that it is not the purpose of this book to replace official security manuals (particularly those in use in government service). Its purpose is to reinforce such manuals and attempt to explain the reasoning behind the security measures prescribed in such manuals.

1.9 Summary

All the security techniques discussed here are complementary to each other. No single technique (e.g., physical security) can, by itself, effect adequate security. There is a great temptation to rely on technical security measures, such as electronic and software security, and to ignore personnel security measures. This would be ineffective as both operators and engineers have the ability to sidestep any technical defenses should they so desire. Good information system security is the balanced mix of all security techniques.

Computer security is not an expensive optional extra which can be bought as a field conversion kit. Computer security has to be designed into an information system from the outset. In particular, the specification, the design and the physical siting of an information system should all be done with the security requirements in mind. If this is not done, the necessary works services required to "improve" security become impractical if not extremely expensive. If the design and the coding of the software are not done with the particular security requirements of the system in mind, any subsequent *proving* that the security requirements of the system have been met will prove to be prohibitively expensive.

The most important security aspect of any information system is personnel security. The motivation and the loyalty of personnel, particularly those with privileged access to the system, have to be assured throughout the life of the system. Technology can assist in keeping the security risks down to a manageable level, but without the active cooperation of all concerned, any security plan is almost useless.

Chapter 2

Technology and Security

In this chapter, there is a discussion of a number of technical computing topics which have a bearing on security. A few of these relate to hardware, but most of them relate to software or a combination of hardware and software. This discussion is not intended to be an introduction to Computer Science, however, it does attempt to explain why certain issues are important for security.

2.1 Privilege and Machine Modes

Most modern computers can run in at least two modes: *user mode* and *privileged mode*. When the computer is running in *privileged mode*, there are no restrictions as to what the program may access in terms of memory, instructions, files and other peripheral devices. When the computer is running in *user mode*, the program will be restricted to the memory and instructions determined by the program last running in *privileged mode*. A program running in *user mode* cannot directly access any files or peripheral devices. If it needs to access a peripheral device, it must make a request to a program running in *privileged mode* to perform the transaction with the peripheral device on its behalf. In almost every case, the program running in *privileged mode* will be an *operating system*.

In a "secure" system there are some essential prerequisites:

- The hardware must support at least two running modes:
  - a *privileged mode* in which there are no restrictions; and
  - a *user mode* in which the program can be prevented from accessing certain memory locations and peripherals, and inhibited from executing certain machine instructions.
- The transition from *privileged mode* to *user mode* must be under the direct control of the privileged program. The transition in the reverse

11

direction must result in the computer being under the control of the original privileged program.

- The computer will leave the *user mode* and revert to *privileged mode* whenever:
  - the *user mode* program makes a request for the *privileged mode* program to perform a privileged operation on its behalf; or
  - the *user mode* program attempts to access an object (memory location or peripheral device) for which it does not have the appropriate access rights or when it attempts to execute a privileged instruction.
- The *privileged mode* program must ensure that the capabilities left for the *user mode* program do not include the ability of the user mode program to change any of its capabilities.

Implicit in these requirements is that privileged programs contain no philosophical design errors or any coding errors. Philosophical correctness is quite frequently a combination of good system design and good administration. For example, in an operating system such as Unix, a user's privileges can be specified in a file; it is therefore essential that, to prevent a user being able to enhance his or her privileges, no user should have write access to such a file.

Privileged programs such as operating systems should treat every privileged service request with extreme caution. It should ascertain whether the requester has the right to request such a service before carrying it out. The majority of "system break-ins" come about as a result of a non-privileged user successfully requesting an operating system to perform a privileged operation on his or her behalf.

There are several examples of systems with and without privileged states and user states and with and without suitable software to exploit these states. At the very simplest level, there is MS–DOS running on a basic Intel 8086 processor: the 8086 processor did not support the concept of privileged states so there was no point in MS–DOS trying to exploit such a mechanism. Later Intel processors, the 80386, the 80486 and the Pentium all support user states and a privileged (supervisor) state; neither MS–DOS nor Windows 3.1 exploit these facilities. Similarly, the Motorola 68000 series of microprocessors supports both states but neither the Macintosh OS7 nor the OS/9 exploit these facilities. The Digital Equipment Corporation (DEC)[1] produces hardware with both states (the VAX[2] computer range and the Alpha range) and operating systems (VMS and Ultrix – a Unix variant) which exploit the protection mechanisms offered by the hardware. In fact, all the Unix variants and look-alikes require hardware with these facilities and exploit them.

---

[1] now owned by Compaq.

[2] VAX computers went out of production during 2000.

2.2 System Configuration

An operating system is usually capable of preventing users from performing illegal operations when the computer system is running normally. Unfortunately there is nothing that software can do to prevent illegal operations taking place when the system is not running. The danger is that when the system is "down", another – less secure – system can be used to bypass security features and make unauthorised changes.

By way of example, it is possible to boot up a PC Unix look-alike operating system called Linux from two floppy discs. Once Linux is up and running, the unauthorised user can login as *root* (the privileged user) and then mount the discs of the operating system normally resident on the hard disc. Then it is a trivial matter to alter the security critical files such as /etc/passwd. When the legitimate version of the operating system is run up, it will be blissfully unaware of the unauthorised changes made to its files.

There are two possible answers to such a threat:

- Keep the system in a secure room so as to prevent any unauthorised users obtaining physical access to the hardware.
- When the system is shut down, calculate sum checks of all security critical files and write them to a floppy disc. The disc should be kept separate from the system in a secure place and reunited with the system when it is next booted so that the operating system can check for tampering with the system files while the system was down. (There is little point in keeping the file sum checks on the hard disc as these can be recalculated after the changes have been made to the files.)

The first of these is always applicable. The second is a requirement only with the most secure systems.

2.3 Physical Aspects of Discs and Tapes

The main difference between discs and tapes is the speed at which data can be accessed. A disc holds its information on the surface of a number of plates coated with iron oxide. The information is accessed by a set of read/write heads (one per plate surface) which can be moved anywhere over the surface of the plates in a short period of time. On the other hand, tapes only have a single set of read/write heads. These are kept still while the tape is moved over the heads. The time taken to access the information is determined by the speed at which the tape can be wound and unwound from its reel. Typically, it takes about 15 minutes to search a tape from one end to the other; this is in contrast to the 200 milliseconds maximum it would take to access any particular piece of information on a hard disc.

2.3.1 Hard Discs

In this section, we will have a close look at how data is held on a hard disc and discuss which factors affect the performance of such a disc.

If you were to break the seals and open up a hard disc drive, you would find the following assemblies:

The disc and motor assembly: usually this consists of up to eight round plates coated in a high quality magnetic film. The plates are all clamped together separated by spacers roughly 2.5mm thick. Not so obvious, there is a small electric motor about 20mm in diameter built into the centre of the stack of plates. The purpose of the motor is to spin the stack of plates at high speed (typically 5400rpm).

The head assembly: in one corner of the casing there will be a shaft onto which is placed a strange comb-like object. The teeth of the comb neatly fit into the spaces between the plates of the disc assembly. On the tips of each of the comb teeth, there should be two tiny sets of read/write heads: one facing up and the other down. These are the means by which data is written to and read from the disc. The head assembly is controlled either by a speech coil mechanism or, in some older discs, by a stepper motor. This control mechanism swings the head assembly about its shaft so that the heads on the tips of the comb teeth can move across the surfaces of the plates.

It should be mentioned that the individual heads are not actually in contact with the data surfaces. They fly aerodynamically a few microns above the surface. The aerodynamic force is generated as a result of the disc surface moving past the heads. Consequently, special arrangements must be made to move the heads to a safe *landing zone* when the power is removed from the disc system and the plates come to a halt. In modern disc systems, this is achieved automatically; however, with most early hard discs, a special program (such as PARK) has to be invoked before power is removed from the disc system so as to ensure that the heads are moved to the landing zone before the plates come to rest. This is quite important as one of the most common causes of disc failure (and loss of data) results from the heads actually coming into physical contact with the data surfaces. Such an occurrence is known as a *disc crash*.

(Do not attempt to open up a working hard disc casing: that will automatically invalidate any guarantee associated with the disc; more significantly, it will allow microscopic dust particles to get into the mechanism. This will cause the recording surfaces of the plates to be damaged irrecoverably as soon as the disc is next turned on.)

If there are n plates then there will be $(2 \times n) - 3$ data surfaces. No use is made of the outer two surfaces and one of the remaining surfaces is reserved for control information. Each data surface is composed of a number

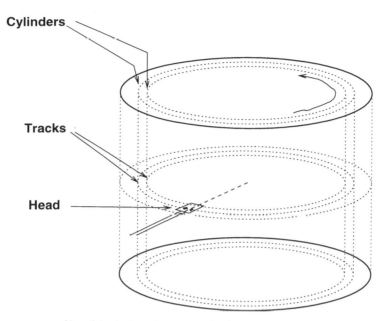

Fig. 2.1: A disc showing cylinders, tracks and heads.

of *tracks*. The tracks are circles concentric with the axis of the plate. The actual separation between each track is very small indeed as a typical plate surface will hold more than 1000 tracks in a band which is about 16mm wide. The head assembly is so arranged that each set of heads is held over a particular track on its respective surface. For example, if there are eight plates, there will be 13 data surfaces (and one control surface) each with its own set of heads over a particular track. This collection of tracks which can be accessed simultaneously (without moving the head assembly) is called a *cylinder*.

Each data track on a disc is composed of a number of *sectors* spread evenly around the track. Between the sectors there will be a small gap which holds more control information. Since the late 1980s, most disc manufacturers have standardised on a sector size of 512 bytes. The size of the gap between sectors, however, can vary from disc type to disc type and is a function of the disc control logic. Typical gap sizes are from 80 to 150 bytes. In practice, 512 bytes is rather small for most practical purposes; consequently, low level software (usually part of the operating system) group (or *Indexcluster*) sectors into *blocks*. Thus an application programmer is totally unaware of 512 byte sectors and writes and reads block size buffers (which may contain 2048, or even 4096 bytes) to and from the disc.

To put this discussion into perspective, let us look at the actual numbers (or *disc geometry* as it is called) of a typical 1 GByte disc. Such a disc will have about 1400 cylinders, 13 data surfaces and each track will have 112 sectors making some 2038400 sectors in all.

The sector is the lowest addressable unit on a disc. The address of any particular sector is specified to the disc control logic in terms of:

Cylinder: that is to say which one of the concentric set of tracks should the head assembly be positioned over;

Surface: i.e., which particular set of data heads should be made active; and

Sector: i.e., which sector in the selected track should be used.

2.3.1.1 Disc Operations. The final aspect of a disc we need to consider is what commands a disc unit is capable of obeying. These are listed below:

Read one or more specified sectors from the disc into a buffer.

Write the contents of a buffer to one or more specified sectors on the disc.

Compare the contents of one or more specified sectors with the contents of a buffer.

Raw Read part of a track into a buffer.

Raw Write a buffer to part of a track.

Seek move the head array to a specified cylinder.

The *Read* command does exactly what it says.

The *Write* command merely copies data from a program data buffer onto a disc. The user level write command is implemented, normally, as a *Write* command followed by a *Compare* command, which effectively implements a read–after–write check.

The *Seek* command is used to move the head array to the required cylinder before a read or write operation can take place.

The *Raw Read* and *Raw Write* commands are reserved for special operations such as formatting the disc. In an operating system such as VMS or Unix, these operations are not made available to normal users; they are reserved for use by the system administrator.

2.3.1.2 Disc Partitions. Modern discs are very large by comparison with the original models which were between 8 and 100 MBytes. In many ways, modern discs are inconveniently large. Some operating systems are incapable of managing discs larger than a certain size; for example, MS–DOS cannot cope with discs larger than 2 GBytes (2×10^9 bytes). Secondly, it may be desirable to separate read/write user data from read only system software. The easiest way to accomplish this would be to put the user data and the system software on separate discs. However, it would be uneconomic (too expensive) to have two physical discs, one of which may be almost empty. Thirdly, some people want more than one operating system to share a a disc — normally this would be impossible as each operating system requires a disc structure specific to it. The solution is to divide the physical disc into a number of logical discs known as *partitions*.

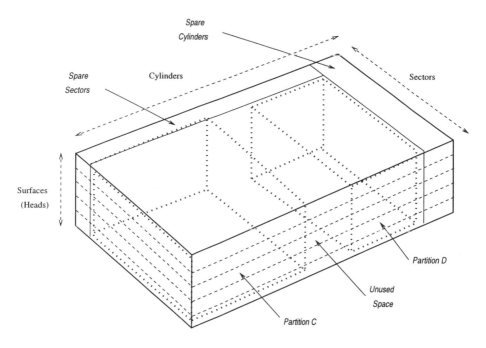

Fig. 2.2: A logical disc structure showing cylinders, tracks, heads, partitions and unused space.

Partitions are defined by entries in a *partition table* held in the first sector of the physical disc. By convention, and in the interests of efficiency, a partition consists of a number of complete cylinders. Each partition table entry holds just sufficient information to define the position of the partition on the physical disc (by specifying the physical cylinder number of the start of the partition), its size (usually expressed as the number of cylinders), and its type.

Figure 2.2 shows the logical structure of a hard disc with two logical partitions. Note that not all the physical disc is available for use by the user. When the disc is physically formatted, a couple of cylinders are reserved to accommodate alternative sectors for unusable sectors in the data partitions. Most operating systems, for reasons of efficiency, group several sectors together to form logical *blocks* (*clusters* in DOS speak); it is normal for logical tracks to consist of whole numbers of blocks. The remaining unused sectors are made to be logically invisible — they can be used by the operating system as substitute sectors for unusable sectors physically within the logical track. Finally, it is quite feasible (but not necessarily useful) for there to be other physical cylinders which are not part of any of the partitions defined on the disc.

In theory, a physical disc may be divided into any number of partitions each of arbitrary size. In practice, most physical discs have between one and four partitions. There are also practical limits to the number of partitions on a physical disc: Unix SCSI discs may have up to 7 partitions (sometimes known as *slices*) and DOS/Windows IDE discs can have as many as 15 partitions.

As far as the applications programmer and the user are concerned, a partition is a logical disc; a virtual disc implemented by the operating system. A partition needs to be initialised to be made into a file system just in the same way as a simple hard disc.

Some discs are not partitioned. Floppy discs are never partitioned as the resulting partitions would be too small to serve any useful purpose. With hard discs, it is very unusual to find partitions smaller than 16 MBytes; MS–DOS disc management utilities will prevent a user from creating a partition smaller than 16 MBytes (as this would require the use of the obsolete "12 bit FAT").

2.3.2 CD–ROMs

Superficially, a CD–ROM is quite similar to a read only hard disc but has only a single recording surface. A CD–ROM consists of a $5\frac{1}{4}$ disc of a clear plastic (known as *lexan*). In fact the disc is a sandwich consisting of a very thin film of aluminium sealed between two sheets of lexan. The information is held in the form of "bumps" or depressions in the aluminium film. The data is read from the disc by shining a laser beam onto the aluminium film and detecting the bumps from the reflections coming back from the aluminium film.

Commercial discs are made by evaporating aluminium onto a moulded lexan surface and then heat sealing in the metallic layer with a second piece of lexan. It is possible to produce similar discs in small quantities by a completely different process. These WORM (Write Once, Read Many) discs consist of a sandwich which includes an additional layer, in contact with the aluminium film which swells when it is illuminated by a beam of infra–red radiation of a particular wavelength. (This wavelength is completely different from the wavelength of the radiation used to read the information from the disc surface.) By shining the beam from an appropriate infra–red laser onto the reflecting surface, the recording layer is made to swell resulting in a depression in the aluminium foil. By switching the write laser on and off at the appropriate times as the disc is spinning, it is possible to record data on the foil surface which can be read back later by a conventional CD–ROM player.

Because CD–ROM technology was developed from the recorded music CD, the data format is somewhat different from that found on a hard disc. For a start, the data is not arranged in cylinders but in one long continuous spiral. Secondly, the data is arranged in 2048 byte data blocks with a further 304 bytes of control information rather than the 512 + 137 bytes normally found on hard discs. In the CD–ROM case, 288 bytes of the control information is used for error detection and correction in such a way that residual undetected errors should be less than one in 10^{13}. Other differences affect the performance of CD–ROMs as compared with hard discs: CD–ROMs rotate significantly slower than hard discs and the head assemblies are rather less nimble than those of hard discs. These factors result in the overall performance of CD–ROMs being about an eighth of that from a hard disc.

The way that data is organised on a CD–ROM is very different to that found on any hard disc. As with music CDs, each CD–ROM starts with a table of contents for up to 99 *tracks*. These *tracks* have nothing to do with the tracks of a hard disc; they are merely ranges of contiguous data blocks on the CD–ROM. These tracks can be looked upon as being analogous to a partition on a hard disc. In practice, normal CD–ROMs usually consist of a single track. As with hard disc partitions, a track is organised into directories and files. As an attempt at true portability, the actual format and structure of a track is defined in the ISO–9660 standard. (Currently, there is only one significant manufacturer that specifies and distributes CD–ROMs in a different format: Apple have a format called HFS for use with MacOS.)

ISO–9660 is a little restrictive as it has to cater for the limitations imposed by MS–DOS and VMS. File names have to conform to the MS–DOS 8.3 format but may be qualified by version numbers (as in VMS). File names may only contain a very limited character set (A–Z,0–9,_); this causes some problems for Unix users. Other restrictions include limiting subdirectories to a depth of 8; there is no support for concepts of ownership, protections or links. As can be imagined, extensions to the ISO–9660 standard have been invented. The most important of these is the Rock Ridge Interchange Protocol (RRIP). Rock Ridge discs conform to the strict ISO–9660 format but include Unix-related file system information hidden away in the ISO–9660 *System Use* area. Unix systems that are aware of RRIP check the *System Use* area for the RRIP signature; if it is found, there will be sufficient information for Unix to reconstruct Unix style file names, ownerships, protections and links.

2.3.3 Floppy Discs

Floppy discs are very similar to hard discs but have the following differences:

- There is only a single plate and that is made of a flexible material such as mylar. Both sides of the plate are used. There is no control surface, consequently the data packing density is very much less than that of a hard disc. This results in a low overall data capacity for a floppy disc, typically 1.4 MBytes.
- The disc (plate) rotates at about one tenth of the speed of a hard disc, thus the performance of floppy discs is very much less than that of hard discs.

- The heads do not fly above the data surfaces but remain in contact with them; this can result, eventually, in wear to both the heads and the data surfaces.
- The disc mechanism is not sealed as is the case for hard discs. There is a mechanical arrangement to allow the disc to be removed from the drive mechanism and replaced by another similar disc. The disc itself is usually protected by a plastic or cardboard envelope.

Because floppy discs do not have a control surface, there is no mechanism for the control logic to confirm which cylinder the heads are currently positioned over. Consequently, the position of the heads has to be calculated from previous head movements. Whenever the system software is uncertain as to the whereabouts of the heads, it has to reposition the head array to cylinder 0 and start again. The first sign of a failing floppy disc is the noise of the heads being retracted and then repositioned several times in succession.

2.3.4 Magnetic Tapes

Magnetic tapes are very different from discs. There are a number of different types of magnetic tape currently in common use:

Half inch open reel tape: this is the industry standard traditional form of magnetic tape. The data is recorded in 9 parallel tracks (one of them reserved for parity). The capacity of such tapes is about 200 MBytes.

6mm QIC cartridges: this form of tape is based on the technology used in aircraft "black box" flight recorders. The data is recorded serially in a single track. There is room on the tape to accommodate 4 data tracks side by side. The capacity of such tapes is typically 150 MBytes.

8mm Exabyte tapes: this form of tape is a miniaturised version of a video cartridge and uses helical recording. The capacity of these tapes can be as much as 25 GBytes.

3mm DAT: this form of tape was originally designed as a high quality audio tape. It never really caught on in the consumer market. It is similar to an Exabyte tape but half the size. The capacity of a standard DAT is about 5 GBytes.

Of these technologies, the best performance is to be had from the traditional open reel tapes; however, this technology suffers from the manpower required to perform the frequent reel changing. The slowest are the QIC tapes. The best compromise in terms of performance and costs is with the Exabyte tapes.

Writing to and reading from magnetic tapes is achieved by moving the tape over a fixed set of heads. A big difference between tapes and discs is that tapes can write arbitrary length data blocks to the tapes. In practice, there is a minimum data block size of about 16 bytes and a practical maximum block size of 64kB. As well as writing data blocks to tapes, it is also possible to write *sentinel blocks* (also known as *tape marks*). These are useful to mark control points on the tape.

2.4 Files and Access Control

Magnetic discs and magnetic tapes are rather special peripherals as they are the means used by computer systems to keep information permanently even when the computer is switched off. They are more complex than other peripherals, such as keyboards and printers, since they may carry data owned by several different users. The nature of the complication lies in the organisation and mechanisms which prevent one user inadvertently accessing or, worse still, corrupting the data belonging to another user. This is achieved as follows:

- The operating system acts as a trusted agent for all users and carries out all operations on discs and tapes on behalf of the users.
- So that both the operating system and the users can keep track of the various collections of data on a disc or tape, the operating system maintains logical named areas of disc (or tape) known as *files*.

Thus the user program can access the files, but it is totally unaware of the disc or tape.

There is a special form of file, known as a *directory*, which contains a list of files together with some system information for each file. In the list of files it is possible to have more directories. In this way, it is possible to make what is commonly called a hierarchical file system. This form of file system is universal with modern operating systems such as Unix, VMS and MS–DOS (see Figure 2.3).

A disc file is a logical collection of disc data blocks. So that an OS can look after a file, it must maintain some housekeeping data about the file. This is usually organised along the following lines:

- Files are usually referred to by a name (e.g., FRED.ADA). The OS keeps lists of file names in special files known as *directories*.
- A *directory* consists of a vector of *file entries*. Each *file entry* normally consists of a file name and an associated *I-node number*. A file can be either a data file or a *subdirectory*.
- An *I-node number* is an index into the *I-node vector*. The *I-node vector* is an array of *I-node entries* held in a reserved area of the filing system.
- An *I-node entry* is a data structure which contains all the information required by the OS for the maintenance of the file.

As has already been indicated, a file system is a hierarchical system of directories and files. A typical file system would look like that shown in

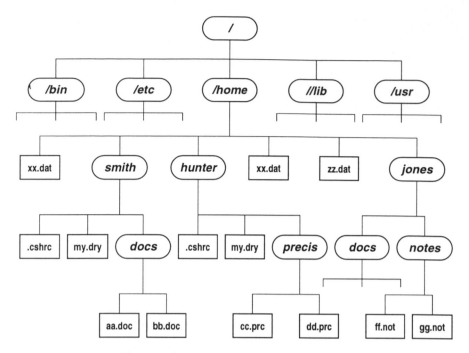

Fig. 2.3: A typical hierarchical file system

Figure 2.3. The file system is basically composed of three classes of object: *leaf files*, *directories* and *I-nodes*. A *leaf file* is a normal file which can contain text (Ada or data) or a program executable binary. A *directory* is a special file listing a number of files "contained" by it, each with its own directory entry. Each directory entry contains the name of the file concerned together with its *I-node number* (which is a pointer to the entry for that file in the *I-node vector* – see Figure 2.4. All the *I-nodes* of a particular file system are held together in a data structure known as the *I-node vector*.

Files themselves consist of a collection of disc blocks – so how does the operating system know which blocks? MS–DOS uses a very simple scheme; VMS and Unix both use a slightly more elaborate (and more flexible) scheme.

VMS and Unix use almost identical systems. Figure 2.4 shows the Unix mechanism in some detail. The directory entry consists only of the file name and a pointer to the *I-node* entry. The I-node entry is a data structure which holds all the information that the operating system has with reference to the file. The most important fields are described below. There are many other fields which are used by the operating system in the efficient administration of the file system.

The *mode* field holds the information which determines the properties of the file. In particular, there is a bit which says whether the file is a directory or just a normal file. Other bits in the mode field determine the access rights

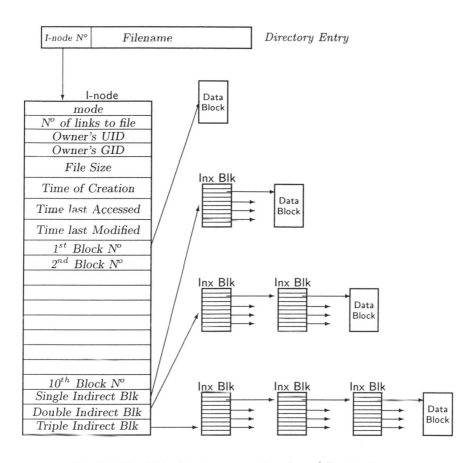

Fig. 2.4: The Unix directory entry, I-node and file structure.

(read, write and execute) for the owner of the file, members of the owning group, and other users.

The contents of most of the other fields are self-explanatory. There are fields that define who is the owner of the file and which group has ownership rights over the file. There are three time fields: the first gives the time that the file was originally created; the second gives the time that the file was last changed and the third gives the time that the file was last read.

Another important field gives the actual size of the file in bytes. This field is important for two reasons: firstly, it determines how many data blocks the file is made up of and, secondly, how much of the last block in the file holds real data. As both Unix and VMS use 32 bit integers, the maximum practical file size is 2 GBytes (2147483647 bytes). (This limit does not apply to the

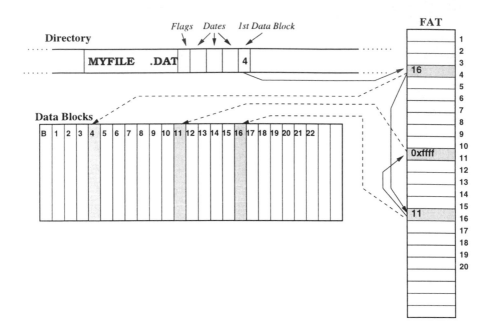

Fig. 2.5: The MS–DOS FAT file structure.

latest releases of Unix SVR4 systems as they now use a 64 bit integer to hold the file size.)

The last important section of the I-node is that which contains the list of data blocks which hold the actual data of the file. In the Unix I-node, only the first 10 entries point directly at data blocks. The eleventh entry points to a block of pointers to data blocks; the twelfth entry points to a block of pointers to blocks of pointers to data blocks. If necessary, there may be a thirteenth pointer using triple indirection to accommodate very large files. VMS does not use indirect pointers to data blocks; when a file is longer than 100 blocks, the list of blocks is continued in continuation I-nodes.

MS–DOS uses a data structure called the *File Allocation Table* (FAT) which consists of a number of cells, one cell for each block in the file system, formed into chains. The directory entry consists of the file name itself, its creation date, some system flags and, finally, the block number of the first logical block of the file. In the corresponding FAT cell there will be the block number of the next logical block and so on. The last logical block is indicated by the value 0xffff in its FAT cell. This mechanism is illustrated in Figure 2.5.

2.4.1 File Access Controls

As the operating system checks and carries out all the operations on discs and tapes on behalf of all users it has full control over which user may access which file; it can even control what sort of access an individual user may have with any file. Multi–user operating systems such as VMS and Unix take advantage of this facility to allow individual users to specify, for a specific file, who may read, write to, delete and execute it.

VMS divides the user population into groups so that every user is a member of one, and only one, group. When a user creates a file, he becomes the owner of the file and the group to which the owner belongs is the group owner. Associated with the file there are four types of permission: *read*, *write*, *execute* and *delete*. The owner can specify the permissions for four sets of people: the *owner* himself, the owner's *group*, the rest of the *world* and the *system* manager. This basic access control scheme can be rather restrictive in a real organisation so VMS offers an additional mechanism known as an *access control list* (ACL). As well as these general permissions, a file can have associated with it a list of other individual users who can have specific access rights to the file which override the general permissions. Thus the VMS file access control mechanisms are sufficiently flexible to cater for almost any requirement.

The Unix file access control system is simpler but somewhat less flexible. In Unix a *user* can be a member of many *groups* simultaneously. However, a file may be only associated with one group. Also with Unix, there is no specific *delete* permission for a file; to be able to delete a file, a user must have write permission for the file itself and, at the same time, write permission for the directory in which the file is located.

The Unix system allows a group to be set up for every "interest group" and allows for the fact that an individual user can be a member of several "interest groups" at the same time. The main limitation of the Unix system is that all the members of a group have the same access rights. This is in contrast to VMS's ACLs which allow for access rights to be specified for each individual user.

To make up for this apparent lack of functionality, some Unix implementations, in particular Sun's Solaris, have recently implemented ACLs as an add on feature to their proprietry file systems.

These mechanisms, flexible as they are, do not satisfy all the requirements of a multi–level secure operating system. In such a system, each user has a *clearance* which defines the maximum sensitivity of information that the user is permitted to access. As well as the users, all peripheral devices are allocated a maximum sensitivity that they are allowed to handle. At the same time, all files are given a sensitivity value. The operating system then has to determine whether a transaction is permitted using the sensitivity of the file and the clearance of the user or peripheral before considering the file permissions.

Such a mechanism is not found in any standard operating system nor can it be implemented in a manner that would satisfy any of the national security agencies by a simple *appliqué* fix. Genuine multi–level secure operating systems tend to be rather expensive. Although superficially they appear to be very similar to the standard version of one of the widely available multi–user operating systems, they are complete rewrites. It has been said that the multi–level version of an operating system bears the same resemblance to the original version as a works rally car to the normal showroom version.

2.5 RAID Storage

In most computer systems, it is the system data which is the most valuable asset; it is also the most vulnerable asset. Historically, the system designer's ingenuity has been expended in contriving elaborate systems to safeguard the system data regardless of any disaster befalling the system. In general, these systems involved both the replication of the data together with complex and manpower-intensive procedures to ensure the high availability of the data and the rapid restoration of the data in any event affecting the online copy of the system data.

In more recent years, the price of hardware, discs in particular, has dropped dramatically. (In 1992/3 the price of a SCSI 1.2 GByte hard drive was about £1600+VAT; the 2000 price is about £140+VAT for a SCSI 9 GByte hard drive, the smallest size widely available. This represents a year on year $\frac{1}{3}$ reduction in price.) In the meantime, the cost of manpower has risen. Hence it is now uneconomic to continue with "traditional" solutions to the data integrity problem. The modern preferred solution is to use lots of hardware in standardised configurations to provide high data availability.

The University of California at Berkeley specified 6 standard configurations of disc drives to provide various combinations of integrity and performance. These systems are known as the *RAID levels*. (RAID stands for "**R**edundant **A**rray of **I**nexpensive **D**iscs"). The term *level* is rather misleading, the term *configuration* would be more appropriate, since a particular level bears no relationship to any of the lower numbered levels.

The six levels are:

RAID level 0 consists of *striping*: typically four, say, disc drives are ganged together so that 2 bits of each data byte are written to each drive. This arrangement can achieve very high data transfer rates to and from disc. However, such an arrangement does not increase the availability of the data.

RAID level 1 consists of *mirroring*: there are two identical sets of discs each with identical copies of the data. This arrangement provides greatly improved data availability: the chances of both sets of data failing at the same time are very low. Provided that the failing disc unit can be identified and replaced quickly, single component failures have a minimal effect on an operational system. There are costs: there has to be at least double the disc capacity to hold the mirror copy and all write/update operations have to be duplicated. There may be performance gains for read operations: if a number of users require simultaneous read access to the data, the load can be split between both halves of the mirror.

RAID level 2 is where a disc farm is supplemented by at least one parity disc, each parity disc holding error correcting data for the data discs. The purpose of the parity disc was that should a data disc go down, it would be possible to replicate the lost information on a replacement disc. The problem with this arrangement lay in the fact that when a data disc was updated, it was also necessary to update the parity disc(s); hence there is some loss of performance over a conventional (unprotected) disc system.

RAID level 3 consists of striping with a parity disc. This arrangement has very little going for it: the parity mechanism adds little to the data integrity over RAID level 0; performance is also down on RAID level 0 because of the additional overhead of the parity disc. This arrangement is not normally available off-the-shelf.

RAID level 4 consists of RAID level 3 without the striping. It suffers from the same disadvantages as RAID level 3 and, consequently, is not available commercially.

RAID level 5 is a combination of striping (RAID level 0) and Error Correcting Codes (ECC). This arrangement is such that should one of the discs fail, a copy of the failed disc could be calculated and constructed on a replacement disc from the information on the remaining serviceable discs. This has the advantage of providing similar performance gains to RAID level 0 and, at the same time, provides a measure of resilience in the event of a single disc failure.

Assuming that the purpose of using RAID is to increase the availability of the data, the only RAID levels worthy of any consideration are levels 1 and 5. If performance is measured in terms of high data transfer rates then a hardware implementation of RAID level 5 would seem to be preferable. If simplicity rather than outright performance is the priority then RAID level 1 should suffice. Discs are now so cheap, the additional costs of full data mirroring are hardly noticeable. There are good software implementations of disc mirroring available, e.g., Sun's `DiscSuite` software.

2.6 Summary

A degree in computing science is not an essential prerequisite for the understanding of computer security. However, there are a number of points which are very pertinent to computer security:

- It is possible to exploit the *privileged mode/user mode* mechanism of many systems to assist in the enforcement of a system security policy.
- The effectiveness of an operating system enforced security policy is critically dependent on the absence of software errors in those modules of the operating system used to enforce the policy.
- No matter how secure an operating system is and how clever the rest of the system software, it can only enforce the policy defined by the humans controlling it. In particular, the policy itself should be protected – users should not be able to change any file the system uses to define or implement the policy.
- A system cannot protect itself when it is turned off or when untrusted personnel are allowed to gain physical access to it.
- Discs and tapes are special peripheral devices which can hold several files owned by several different users. It is important to deny to normal users any form of direct access to such devices. Equally, it is important to protect all discs and tapes from any physical access by untrusted personnel.
- Any security policy which the software is called upon to implement must be compatible with the capabilities of the software.

Chapter 3

Physical Security

The purpose of physical security is to separate people who are not authorised to access certain sensitive objects from those objects. In general, this is achieved by a combination of hiding the whereabouts of the sensitive objects and then enclosing the objects in a protective container so as to make it difficult to gain access to the objects even if their whereabouts is known.

Physical security is very important for a number of reasons:

- Computer hardware is very attractive to the less honest members of society. Some components, particularly memory SIMMs and DIMMs, can be worth more than their weight in gold.
- If hackers can get physical access to a computer system, they can very easily bypass most technical security precautions. Consequently, unless investment in technical protection is matched by investment in appropriate security measures, the investment is wasted.
- Backup tapes and discs deserve effective physical protection. One of the more ingenious methods of perpetrating a computer fraud is for an employee to tamper with backup tapes (for example, to increase a current account balance) and then to provoke a system disc crash. The doctored backup tape is used to restore the file system. The advantage of using this method is that it bypasses any online audit mechanism.

There is a public misconception that all protective containers should be impregnable and constructed like Fort Knox. Such an approach is rarely sensible or cost-effective. Normal good practice is to use a container which is sufficiently resistant to opening that anyone attempting to gain illegal access to it would either attract the attention of the police or would be still at the scene of the attempted crime when the next periodic security patrol visits the area. There is some additional merit in making the container appear to be impregnable as that, in itself, could discourage many would-be attackers.

If we abandon the concept of the Fort Knox approach, physical security becomes a combination of security personnel and physical barriers to protect sensitive assets. The prime purpose of the physical barriers, walls, fences, safes, etc. is to buy time for the security personnel to arrive at the location to provide the necessary protection of the assets. The effectiveness of any barrier is measured in the time required to circumvent it.

The best physical security comes in layers. The most common example of such security is the traditional four layers:

1. The site perimeter fence with a guard house at the point of entry;
2. Controlled access to individual buildings;
3. Locked office doors; and
4. a locked safe within an office.

Administered with common sense, such a system provides adequate protection for most information. The main threats to such a system are sloppy procedures and irresponsible use of pass-keys. It should not be possible for an individual to get from the public side of the perimeter fence into a safe in an office without the assistance of another member of staff. If an employee loses his keyring which then finds its way into hostile hands, it should not be possible for an unauthorised person to get access to the contents of any safe.

In the design of the physical security precautions, there are a number of simple principles that need to be taken into account:

- Wherever possible, barriers should be in full view of security personnel, either directly or by the use of closed-circuit TV cameras. Thus chain link fencing is normally preferable to solid walls as attackers should be seen sooner with the former.
- In general, defence should be in depth; thus two simple barriers would be more effective than a single, more elaborate, barrier costing the same price.
- Barriers should be designed to withstand attacks from both the inside as well as the outside. This is to impede the escape of an attacker surprised on the job.
- The layout of barriers inside the outer perimeter should be such as to channel attackers and escapers towards observation posts.
- The overall layout of the site should allow security patrols to get to any part of the site within the "protection time" of the outermost perimeter.

It is realised that these principles amount to counsels of perfection and may be impossible to implement in particular cases. However, they can still be used as a guide when deciding how and where to make security investments.

Physical security is one of those areas which need to be considered from the very start of a project if security costs are to be kept down. The retrofitting of physical security measures can be very expensive indeed.

The rest of this chapter is devoted to the application of physical security to information systems.

3.1 The Security Domains

It is convenient to divide the site into a number of domains or zones:

- The Global Security Environment (GSE),
- The Local Security Environment (LSE),
- The Electronic Security Environment (ESE).

These domains are deliberately rather vague and general. This is to allow the basic principles to be applicable to a wide variety of circumstances. The general nature of the GSE and the LSE is illustrated in Figure 3.1 below, which uses, by way of an example, an out-of-town supermarket.

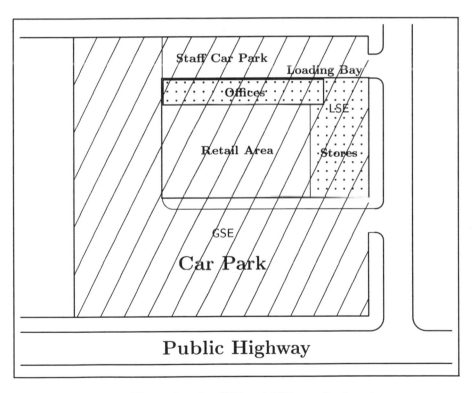

Fig. 3.1: Illustrating the GSE and LSE security domains.

3.1.1 The Global Security Environment

The GSE consists of that area over which the organisation can exert some form of control or influence. Typically, this will extend up to the perimeter fence of an establishment. However, in some circumstances it can even extend beyond the perimeter fence if the ground outside the perimeter is under observation and the establishment has the ability to influence the behaviour of the general public on that ground by, for example, calling for the police to intervene in a situation. Taking a shop as an example, the GSE will extend to the front doors and, possibly, to that part of the pavement overlooked by the shop windows. In an out-of-town shopping mall, the GSE will cover the shop premises and the immediately adjacent parking area (see Figure 3.1).

Security within the GSE usually consists of the siting of vehicle parking and general precautions against vandalism and theft (including pilfering and shoplifting). Quite frequently, there are the minimum of checks on people and vehicles entering and leaving the GSE. However, it is good practice to limit the number of gates (access points) into and out of the GSE so that, in the event of an incident, it is a relatively simple matter to impose a checking system.

There should be someone nominated to be responsible for security within the GSE, together with a clear policy stating which activities are permissible within the GSE and which are strictly prohibited. Enforcement of this security policy is usually carried out by some form of security guard force with the cooperation and backing of the establishment staff.

3.1.2 The Local Security Environment

The LSE is that part of the premises over which you would hope to achieve complete control. In the example of a shop, the LSE would normally extend to include the area behind the shop counters and any offices and store rooms at the back of the shop. In general, it consists of those areas to which the management would wish to restrict access to known and trusted individuals.

Normally, the management keeps a tally of who enters and leaves the LSE. In larger organisations, it is normal practice for a formal record to be kept of all visitors to the LSE. This record can then be used for two purposes: firstly, it is a record against which the visits of individuals can be checked for some enquiry at some time in the future and, secondly, it can be used to determine that all visitors have left the premises by the end of normal office hours.

Within the LSE itself, there may well be different zones covering work areas of differing degrees of sensitivity. These zones can be either hierarchal or separate or even a combination of both. In particular, it is normal practice for the suite of rooms containing large computer systems and their associated communications equipment to form a special zone within the LSE. This special zone is normally used to restrict the people who may have intimate contact with the equipment of which the main elements of the information system is comprised to the essential operations staff. Any visitors to this special zone are normally accompanied by an escort.

3.1.3 The Electronic Security Environment

The ESE consists of that part of the system (and premises) which forms part of the information system. Because the information system is incapable of defending itself against the knowledgeable and determined attacker, the ESE should reside entirely within the LSE. The ESE includes the computer system together with all of its peripherals, terminals and communications interfaces. The security measures used to protect the ESE itself are all technical and are discussed in Chapter 5 and Appendix C.

3.2 Security Aspects of Layout

Physical security measures should extend to the layout of the computer site. It is unwise to allow a computer centre to be situated immediately bordering onto a car park. Such a situation would permit at least two unwanted dangers:

1. It would be possible to threaten the computer centre with a car bomb.
2. It would be possible for an unfriendly agent to place sophisticated electronic monitoring equipment very close to the computer system, thereby possibly illegally extracting information from the system.

Layout of the site also encompasses the layout of communications equipment and cables (which form part of the ESE) – items often overlooked. All communications equipment should be inaccessible to all but those who have a specific need to access it. Modern "bugging" devices are very small, easy to install and very difficult to notice in a casual inspection. Cables are also vulnerable. It used to be the accepted practice for all cabling to be hidden, away out of sight, in ducting. The problem with this approach was that it was almost impossible to see whether the cabling had been tampered with. The modern approach is to place all the cabling on walls in public places (e.g., running along a busy corridor just above door height) so that any attempt to tamper with them would be difficult to hide.

3.3 Summary

No amount of technical ingenuity will replace physical security. It is important to ensure that only authorised people are allowed access to a computer system. Further, it is prudent that physical security measures should ensure that potentially hazardous items cannot be taken into the computer area (e.g., bombs) and that classified items cannot be taken off the site without due authority. Most physical security measures need to be supplemented by sensible procedures particularly in the areas of human patrolling and the handling of keys.

Chapter 4

Personnel Security

The principles of personnel security with computer systems do not differ from those with any other sort of system. However, the high technology aspects of computer systems can make the problem worse than with conventional systems. Visitors attracted to a computer system because of the novelty value of a computer should rapidly disappear as a problem. Even so, it is wise to view all visitors with cynical suspicion: do not allow them to "have a go" on an operational system and, if possible, try to avoid allowing them to touch or handle any of the operational equipment - no matter how important they may seem to be!

Programmers and engineers are a particular threat to computer systems. This is because it is impossible for the gate-keeper (guard or MoD policeman) to detect whether the software entering the site on a magnetic tape or the printed circuit board in the boot of the engineer's car has been tampered with. One has to rely on these people adhering to the strictest of security procedures off the site as well as on the site. It is possible to insist on contractors only using named people for support engineers and programmers. This is particularly important with installations which handle very sensitive information. When a computer breaks down, all the sophisticated software security precautions break down with it. The engineers and programmers brought in to effect a repair will be able to see (indeed, may **have** to see) the information present in the machine at the time of the "crash".

4.1 Assessing Personnel Trustworthiness

In order that the implications of personnel security on an IT system can be studied, we need some objective criteria for estimating the trustworthiness of the people. There are many factors which interact to determine a person's motivation. There are many different professions that claim to be able to provide an insight into a person's trustworthiness. All the discussions are very interesting and may provide helpful criteria at some time in the future; however, what is needed is a rough and ready metric which is simple and cheap to administer.

Personnel security, contrary to popular belief, is not a matter of total surveillance of the subject(s). It consists of attempting to determine whether the subject is responsible and not vulnerable to pressure (blackmail). From this, one can make an estimate as to the trustworthiness of the subject. Factors which increase a subject's trustworthiness are:

- The length of time that the subject has been known either to his superiors or to others trusted by his superiors. Thus someone whose personal history is traceable from the time he or she left school is more likely to be trustworthy than some one who has been known for a few weeks.
- The subject has a happy and stable family background and appears to have a stake in the local community.

On the other hand, there are a number of factors which may detract from the subject's trustworthiness:

- if the subject is or has ever been in financial difficulty. There is a risk that the subject may put financial gain before his or her loyalty to the business.
- if the subject has or has ever had proclivities which may make him or her vulnerable to pressure.
- if the subject is or has ever been a member of a fanatical or extremist organisation; this increases the risk that the subject may put the interests of this other organisation before those of the business.
- if the subject has a significant financial interest in a rival organisation there may be a conflict of interest.

In this chapter, it is proposed to set out a simple five point scale of trustworthiness. The justification of such a simple model of trustworthiness is that any more elaborate scale would be spurious. The list below represents an increasing scale of trustworthiness.

P0: the general public – nothing is known of them as individuals, so it is impossible to assign any level of trust.

P1 : customers under some supervision – again relatively little is known about these people as individuals; however, the element of supervision allows intervention to take place before a minor breach of security is allowed to get out of hand. Pupils at a school or students at a university come into this category.

P2: permanent employees – something is known about these people particularly if any employment references were properly followed up. Such people are normally subjected to some form of reliability check. Not only is something known about these individuals, it is also possible to apply quite drastic sanctions against such people, should they commit serious breaches of security.

P3: trusted employees – a lot is known about such people: they have been associated with the organisation for a minimum of five years, say, and they have a stake in the local community, e.g., a house and possibly a mortgage.

P4: highly trusted associates – these people are known personally by the senior management of the organisation and are very likely to have a personal stake in the organisation.

Unfortunately, life is not as simple as that. There are very few organisations who find it cost-effective to employ all the computer specialists they need. The majority of organisations buy in specialist skills such as software consultants, programmers and maintenance engineers. The problem arises in that it is extremely difficult to estimate the trustworthiness of these casual specialists. The best that one can achieve is to contract with the service suppliers that only nominated consultants and engineers can be used and that all such consultants should have undergone equivalent trustworthiness assessment procedures to those of normal employees of the business.

4.2 Example and Leadership

The vetting process described in the previous section is the negative side of personnel security. Important as the vetting process is, it is not sufficient to achieve good security. Ultimately, the quality of the security within an organisation is dependent on the attitudes of the individual members of the organisation towards security. Positive attitudes towards security are to a large extent dependent on the example and leadership shown by the management of the organisation towards security.

Perhaps the most important aspect of personnel security in an organisation is the leadership persuading the staff to take a positive attitude towards all aspects of security. This is relatively easy in a military environment since the safety, and even the survival, of a military unit is often dependent on the maintenance of good security. In a commercial organisation it will need a conscious effort on the part of management to ensure that security is important and that the various security measures and procedures are relevant to the threats and constitute a necessary part of the operational activities of the business.

It is a common misconception that security is the responsibility of the security specialists who can maintain the integrity of the organisation while the real players get on with the main business of the organisation. Everybody has the responsibility to implement the security policy and it is the responsibility of the management to ensure that everyone has the right attitude.

The role of the security specialist is to advise the management on how to minimise the security risks.

The worst possible risk is the example of the boss who claims that the security policy applies to everybody but him. *"Do as I say, not as I do!"*

4.3 Awareness

Security is not an end in itself, although one could be forgiven for thinking so if the majority of literature on the subject is to be believed. All useful security is a defence against one or more specific threats. Security measures and procedures are far more likely to be effective if the personnel involved know about, and understand, these threats. Thus an important aspect of personnel security is the education of all personnel as to the security risks and the appropriate countermeasures.

Part of this is briefing everyone on the security situation and providing credible answers to questions of the sort, *"Why do we have to do...?"* Obviously it may not always be possible to answer such questions; the decision as to whether it would be right to provide the answer is a matter of judgement between the risk of a security breach due to information being too widely disseminated on the one hand, and, a well-informed and motivated workforce on the other.

The workforce will never have a positive attitude to security if the answer to any query is of the form, *"Well, that is what it says in the book!"* Questions should be handled in a constructive manner. They should be looked upon as an opportunity to improve procedures and to do away with unhelpful practices.

Much of good security consists of the workforce acting responsibly. Treating the workforce as if they were truculent children will result in some members of the workforce endeavoring to get their own back, usually through irresponsible acts, which may result in breaches of security. If individuals are treated as if they are trustworthy and responsible, the workforce is more likely to act in a responsible manner.

4.4 IT Staff

In any IT system, there are many personnel with several differing roles. The majority of the people involved are users; these people tend to be held at arm's length by the system. Provided that the system software has been specified and implemented appropriately, the users' access to data and system facilities should be limited to those to which they are entitled. However, the same cannot be said for the system managers, designers, programmers and administrators.

The general threat posed by the technically qualified technical staff is that they can access, modify or destroy any information held by an IT system. The main counter to this threat is some form of "double manning". The principle is that if someone commits a breach of security, it should not go unwitnessed. There is an assumption that collusion cannot be maintained unnoticed for any length of time.

The designers and programmers can constitute a threat to an IT system as they have both the ability and the opportunity to insert the means to circumvent any specified technical security mechanisms. As a consequence, such people need to be screened to one of the higher levels of trustworthiness. Further, these people should never be allowed unsupervised access to the system itself.

System managers and administrators pose a threat to a system mainly because they have physical access to all parts of the IT system. With physical access and a little knowledge, it is possible to bypass any technical safeguard. People employed in these roles need to be cleared to the highest levels of trustworthiness, and in the case of the more sensitive systems, they should never have sole access to the system.

4.5 New Recruits and Leavers

There is yet one more complication: employees are not permanent features of a business. Existing employees grow old and retire or they leave to go to another enterprise as a part of career development; some, even, are found to be unsuitable and are sacked. Management of this turbulence is yet another security problem for the managers.

New recruits need to be briefed and supervised until they know their way around and their trustworthiness can be fully assessed. All new recruits should receive a security briefing from an appropriate level of manager. Such a briefing serves two purposes: it should impart to the recruit that the organisation takes security seriously and, secondly, it should serve to remind management that security is their responsibility and not the responsibility of the security experts.

Secondly, management should prepare a simple document summarising the duties and responsibilities of all personnel towards security. This document should be brief and to the point. It should be, if possible, restricted to one side of A4 and should emphasise no more than the six most important points. It should be suitable for handing to all new recruits; there is no point in expecting them to read a company security manual 200 pages long.

When employees leave the organisation, there should be a standard procedure to debrief them and ensure as far as possible that their departure does not increase the risk to the organisation. This procedure should include:

- An interview with an appropriate manager to thank the leaver for his services to the organisation and to remind him (or her) of his (or her) continuing obligations to the organisation's security, even when he (or she) is no longer employed by that organisation.
- The leaver's computer accounts should be frozen (disabled) and backed up. The files might provide useful evidence in some future security investigation.
- The leaver's privileges should be withdrawn. The leaver should be asked to surrender all keys, electronic access devices and passes.
- Provision should be made to forward the leaver's personal mail and e–mail to a destination of the leaver's choice.

4.6 General

The Metropolitan Police Force (the police force for Greater London) Fraud Squad have compiled a list of indicators which characterise individuals most likely to be involved in fraudulent activity. This list includes the following:

- working excessive hours,
- having a dominating and overbearing personality,
- unwillingness to delegate responsibility to subordinates,
- some form of stress in the subject's private life, for example a seriously ill parent or the break-up of a close relationship.

It must be stressed that just because somebody has one or more of these characteristics, or even all of them, he (or she) is not necessarily guilty of fraud. It does mean, however, that such a person may need additional supervision to keep any threat to organisation under control.

The importance of this aspect of information security is emphasised by the Metropolitan Police estimate that more than 80% of all commercial information system security breaches are committed by employees or contractors of the organisation owning the IT system.

4.7 Summary

There are a number of aspects of personnel security which need to be followed up. The most obvious point is the assessment of the trustworthiness of all those coming into contact with an information system. The next point is that the same people need to be briefed on the threats to the system and the countermeasures to those threats. Finally, these same people need to be motivated to safeguard the security of the system: this is best achieved by a combination of example and leadership.

Chapter 5

Communications Security

It is almost unheard of nowadays to have a completely isolated computer system. Nearly all computer systems in any organisation are linked together by a communications subsystem to form a corporate information system. The communications subsystem brings with it a new set of threats:

- The communication channels (cables, radio shots[1] or even satellite links) are vulnerable to passive "tapping" (i.e., listening to the communications).
- Unauthorised users can tap into a communications subsystem and masquerade as a *bona fide* user.
- The communications software can be subverted and allow unauthorised users access to system resources.

The communications subsystem contains most of the technical security problems in any information system. Consequently, this chapter is the longest in this book by a long way. The use of the Internet brings with it yet another set of problems; these are covered in a separate chapter on the Internet. We will start by considering the actual communications and following on with the services which make direct use of the communications.

To mount an attack on most communications systems (especially those which do not use radio), the attacker has to have physical access to the communications equipment. Anyone with access to the cables can pick up the signals on the cables. (If they were optical fibres, this would be rather less likely.) The real dangers arise when attackers gain access to the communications equipment at the ends of cables and repeaters along communications routes. So, even with communications, all the standard physical security precautions apply.

Physical protection of long cable runs poses a much greater problem. Regular patrolling of cable routes would be prohibitively expensive for a

---

[1] Overland microwave radio relay

government organisation and totally impractical for a commercial concern. For the security of the cables, one has to rely on communications suppliers (in the UK, companies such as BT and Mercury) hiding physical circuits in their communications networks, and, the honesty and trustworthiness of their employees.

Should an attacker gain access to almost any part of the communications system, there are a number of quite sophisticated attacks which can be mounted:

- From a passive tap, one can derive quite a lot of useful user information. Over and above that, if the whole dialogue can be recorded, it may be possible to deduce passwords — either in clear or in an encrypted form! Such an attack is made fairly simple by the use of *sniffer software* packages (which can be downloaded from the Internet).
- Even if the electronic dialogue is encrypted, it is possible to record and deduce the correct responses to an authentication sequence which can then be reused at some later date when attempting to masquerade as a *bona fide* user (this form of attack is known as a *replay* attack).
- Once an unauthorised user has been authenticated, it may be possible for such a user to browse round the system and thus gain access to information to which he or she is not entitled. Worse still, such a person can implant false data into the system or modify existing data.

Such are the potential problems posed by these threats, the UK Government's policy on this matter is simple and straightforward:

- If a computer system, or network, handles any information classified RESTRICTED or above, then it may not be directly connected to any other system, or network, which is not suitably protected.
- If any part of a system, or network, carries any information classified RESTRICTED or above, and it is accessible from uncontrolled areas (e.g., the public telephone network), it must be protected by approved methods of encryption.

These measures are often sufficient to reduce the risks of a successful attack from outside the system to an acceptable minimum. However, these methods are far from being the panacea that they are, all too frequently, made out to be. In the sections that follow, some of the more obvious threats to communications will be examined together with some measures to counter these threats.

5.1 Encryption and Cryptanalysis

It is possible to prevent a third party from prying into the contents of messages being sent electronically by the process of *encrypting* them. This involves the sender processing the message before transmitting it and the receiver reversing the process at the far end so that it can be understood by the recipient. There are a great number of possible encryption mechanisms, however, most of them have practical problems associated with them. It is not the purpose of this chapter to provide the reader with a comprehensive discussion on the subject of codes and ciphers. The purpose of this section is to indicate how and where crypto techniques can help IT security and where their use might be inappropriate. If you need to know more, you should read a good introductory text on the subject such as Simson Garfinkel's "Pretty Good Privacy" [15].

For the purposes of this book, there are two practical mechanisms:

Symmetric encryption: where both the sender and the receiver share a secret key which controls the encryption process. The sender uses the key to encrypt the message and the receiver uses the same key to decrypt the message at the far end.

Asymmetric encryption: where the sender uses one secret key to encrypt the message before sending it and the receiver uses a different secret key to decrypt the received message.

Symmetric encryption is relatively simple to implement and can bo of fected at quite high speeds. However, there are problems associated with symmetric encryption: the main one is that the secret key needs to be known both by the sender and the receiver; this involves some administration to ensure that both ends have the same key. The second problem is that if a third party obtains a copy of the key, the third party has the ability to decrypt and read the message.

Asymmetric encryption requires much more computing power than symmetric encryption and is not really suitable (for the moment) for online en cryption. However, it has a number of other applications beside the protection of messages in transit and it is rather simpler to administer the secret keys than in the case of symmetric encryption.

5.1.1 Crypto Administration

With traditional symmetric encryption there is the problem of ensuring that both parties trying to communicate have identical keys and that these keys are kept secure, away from any third party who would like to listen in on the communication. The administrative process is relatively straightforward when there are only a few individuals who wish to exchange encrypted information. If there are n people wanting to communicate securely, the number of keys required is $\frac{n(n-1)}{2}$ so when the number of individuals wishing to communicate securely rises to about 1000, the number of keys needed is about half a million! This would require a huge administrative support system for it to be maintained for any length of time.

In practice, the demand for keys is not as bad as the general case cited here might imply; even with populations as small as 1000, not everybody wishes to communicate with everybody else. If we were to assume that an individual wishes to communicate directly with only up to 24 others, then only $40 \times 24 \times 23$ keys (i.e., 22080) are needed. This is still a major administrative problem.

Now consider an asymmetric cryptographic system. The most widely used asymmetric cryptographic system is the *Rivest, Shamir* and *Adelman* public key cipher (also known as the RSA system). The way in which the RSA system works is as follows: to encrypt and decrypt a message requires two related keys – P and Q, say. The sender encrypts the message with the key P and the receiver decrypts the message using the second key Q. The integrity of the system relies on the fact that Q is impossible to deduce from P, or the process would be so expensive as to be not worthwhile. The beauty of the system relies on the fact that only the possessor(s) of the key Q has the ability to decrypt messages encrypted using the key P. This lends itself to a practical system where any individual (*Alice*, say) can select such a related pair of keys, place one of them in the public domain and keep the other private. Anybody wishing to send a private message to *Alice* needs only to consult a public repository to find *Alice*'s public key and use it to encrypt the message before sending it to *Alice*. When *Alice* receives the message, she uses her private key to decrypt the message. Such a system is relatively easy to administer, even for large communities, as it only requires $2 \times n$ keys in total.

The RSA system does have a weakness in that a rogue can substitute his public key for *Alice*'s in the public repository. The rogue would then be able to use his private key to decrypt any messages he had intercepted addressed to *Alice* and *Alice* would not be able to decrypt them at all. To combat this threat, one should only use first-hand copies of public keys obtained from trustworthy public repositories.

It would be nice to have a system which combined the simplicity and speed of a symmetric encryption system with the ease of administration of the RSA system. The Diffie–Hellman system allows such a compromise. In this arrangement, two players, *Alice* and *Bob*, wishing to have a private dialogue need to start by exchanging keys. (It is thought to be prudent that *Alice* should use one key to protect information being sent to *Bob* and that *Bob* should use a different key to protect information being sent to *Alice*.) The Diffie–Hellman process is an RSA-like procedure which allows *Alice* and *Bob* to send short messages to each other without the rest of the world being able to deduce what is going on. Such a process is sometimes known as an *Oblivious Transfer Protocol* or OTP.

The actual process relies on very sophisticated mathematics, however, the following illustration indicates how the exchange is effected. (This tale has been ascribed to a number of historic figures including Sir Francis Drake and Queen Elizabeth I.) The system requires a box (chest or briefcase) which can have two padlocks; if at least one padlock is secured to the box, the contents of the box are inaccessible. Thus if *Alice* needs to send a valuable item to *Bob*, say, without the rest of the world being aware of it, she puts the item into the box and secures it with a padlock for which only *Alice* has the key. She then sends the box to *Bob*. When *Bob* receives the box, he cannot open it since he does not possess a key for *Alice*'s padlock; so he adds a second padlock for which only he has a key and then sends the box, now with two padlocks, back to *Alice*. When *Alice* gets the box back, she removes her padlock using her key and then sends the box, now with only one padlock, back to *Bob*. Finally, when *Bob* receives the box for the second time, he can unlock his padlock using his key, thereby gaining access to the contents of the box.

Using two separate boxes (or the one box used twice) *Alice* and *Bob* can exchange keys. These keys can then be used for the exchange of data protected using standard symmetric encryption. At the end of the conversation (session), the keys can be forgotten (safely destroyed). The next time *Alice* and *Bob* wish to have a secure dialogue, they must go through the same process all over again with a fresh pair of keys.

5.1.2 Encryption Weaknesses

It might be thought that by encrypting messages it would be impossible for anyone without the necessary equipment and key settings to be able to read those messages. That might have been the case if it were not for the science of cryptanalysis. Cryptanalysts exploit weaknesses in the encoding procedures and methods which can enable them to deduce the keys and decrypt the messages. There are two main weaknesses in any electronic encryption:

- Perfect encryption is effected by combining the original *plain text* with a random bit sequence. Unfortunately, the electronically generated random bit sequences used in cryptography are only pseudo-random (i.e., after a large number of bits the "random" sequence will repeat (or cycle). If a listening cryptanalyst can detect a cycling bit stream, it can lead to the code being broken.
- Perhaps the greatest threat to a crypto system is when a cryptanalyst can compare the plain text with the corresponding encrypted bit pattern. Nearly all messages (certainly all military messages) have standard preambles and postambles. If the listening cryptanalyst can determine the message start and end he is in a position to compare possible plain texts with the encrypted bit stream. This is another opening for a cryptanalyst to break the cipher and deduce the original plain text.

It is possible to prevent a pseudo-random bit sequence from appearing to cycle by using a very large cycle, i.e., a very large number of bits before the bit sequence (typically more than 10^9 bits) is allowed to repeat. Then only a very small fraction of the cycle (e.g., less than $\frac{1}{16}$) is used, and the key is reset and a new cycle is started. Thus in a crypto system, a key setting has a "life" measured in the number of bits encrypted. The actual length of this life will depend on the characteristics of the particular system in use. It is because of the correlation between a particular cipher mechanism and its life that the actual life of a cipher should be a well guarded secret. In a communications network of any size, it is essential that there are procedures which cause key changes to take place quickly and simultaneously at both ends of a communications link at regular intervals.

There are several measures which can be taken to prevent an attacking cryptanalyst from being able to match encrypted bit patterns with the corresponding plain text. The most effective method, when it can be used, is to pump a continuous encrypted stream from end to end of a communications channel so that it is impossible to detect where a message starts or finishes. There is a danger associated with the continuous encrypted bit steam; that is, if the space between actual messages is represented by the same recurring plain text bit pattern, this can give an attacking cryptanalyst an insight into the nature of the pseudo–random bit stream used in the encryption process. Consequently, the plain text of the fill should be a stream of characters such that it is impossible to recognise a real message embedded in the fill.

There are situations in which the use of a continuous stream of encrypted data is not appropriate. The most important of these are half duplex communication systems, such as net radio and packet switched networks.

In the case of net radio, the normal practice, in plain text, is to use a fixed header and trailer to each transmission. When the transmission is encrypted, the header and trailer should not be encrypted (quite apart from the lead it would give the attacking cryptanalyst, there is no point). Where the body of the message is known to have a fixed format, it is advisable to disguise this in some way, for instance, by folding the message – splitting it, then transmitting the second part immediately before the first part. All small messages, such as acknowledgements, should be disguised by the use of padding.

Packet switched networks pose an even greater problem. Each packet normally consists of a header (supplied by the network) and a body containing the data. If the whole packet is encrypted for transmission between nodes, the receiving node is forced to decrypt the packet so that it can determine how to dispose of the packet. The danger resulting from this is that the communications node will contain a plain text version of the body of the packet. Thus the node will require the full physical protection appropriate to the sensitivity of the body of the message.

The alternative is to leave the header *in clear* and to encrypt the packet body only. This leaves some potentially sensitive information totally unprotected, in particular:

- the packet type;
- the source and destination of the packet; and, possibly
- any sequencing information associated with the packet.

A compromise can be achieved by encrypting the data together with any associated transport level protocol envelope and leaving any network layer and data link layer headers *in clear*. Again, to make life more difficult for the attacker, all purely protocol packets should be padded out and disguised to resemble normal data packets. When long messages are sent split into several packets, the constituent packets of the message should be fed into the network in a random order. In a network carrying transaction traffic (i.e., bursts of traffic sustained only through the life of a transaction) it may be desirable to disguise the transactions by the inclusion of dummy packets.

5.2 Authentication Dialogues

If an attacker gains access to the communications he may not be content with monitoring traffic to obtain information. If he can usurp a genuine user's identity he may be able to persuade the system to output to him precisely the data he is looking for. Worse still, he may be able to persuade the system to accept erroneous data, possibly in the execution of a fraud. One approach to this is hacking (see the section on hacking below). There are two other methods of achieving the same result:

- An attacker can monitor the dialogue between a genuine user and the system, including the authentication sequence. Then, at some later time, the attacker can gain "legitimate" access to the system by repeating the dialogue. This is known as a *replay attack*.
- Alternatively, an attacker can monitor a circuit and wait until a *bona fide* user has completed his authentication dialogue; then the line to the real user is disconnected and the attacker's terminal is substituted for that of the real user. This is called a *switch attack*.

The defence against the replay attack is achieved using time dependent authentication techniques. These make use of keys shared only by the two participants, time stamping and strict packet sequence numbering. Unless a third party knows the shared authentication key, he cannot generate the necessary valid encoded authentication field in every data packet, thus a recipient can readily determine the authenticity of every packet. The inclusion of the time stamp in the field ensures that the data packet is valid for only a short time; this, combined with the packet sequencing, guards against any replay attack. For a rather fuller discussion of the threats and countermeasures, the reader is referred to Section 5.3.

There is no real technological antidote to the switch attack. The primary defence against such an attack has to be physical security. Such an attack is far more difficult to effect if the communications media is fibre optics rather than copper cable. Attempts have been made to counter this threat by the use of frequent polling of user terminals. Should a terminal fail to respond to a poll, the assumption is that the terminal has been disconnected during the first stage of a switch attack. Even if the polling is confined to those terminals actually logged in, the administrative overheads of checking out false alarms due to genuine intermittent communications will, almost certainly, nullify any useful effects of the polling. Worse still, if there are a large number of terminals, all being polled about twice every second, the effect will be a severe degradation of the communications.

5.2.1 Crypto Signatures

It would be very useful if it were possible to provide some form of unforgeable digital signature which could be used as an authority for some transaction to take place, for example, the digital equivalent of a manual signature on a cheque. Such a system can be implemented by the signatory encrypting the statement to be signed using his RSA private key. Anyone wishing to verify the signed statement has to decrypt the "signature" using the signatory's public key. If the "signature" decrypts to his name then the "signature" has to be genuine since only the signatory has access to his private key.

   These techniques have been generalised so as to cater for situations where more than one signature from a set of signatories is required to permit a transaction to take place. This corresponds to a situation where two signatures of board members are required on company cheques with a monetary value greater than a preset amount. The principle behind the implementation of such a system can be described as follows:

- suppose the total population of possible signatories is d, and r signatures are required to authorise a transaction;
- the signatory population can be represented by d–dimensional space;
- the authorisation figure is represented by an r–dimensional subspace in the $(d-1)$–dimensional space; such a figure is uniquely specified by d points;
- each signatory is represented by a point in the $(d-1)$–dimensional subspace;

   For example, suppose we have a pool of four signatories and two signatures are required to authorise a transaction. The authorisation figure will be a line in 4–dimensional space. All the signatures will consist of a point on the authorisation line. Any two points on this line are sufficient to define it; thus any two signatories can define this line thereby providing the necessary authorisation.

5.2.2 Summary

Encryption can afford some protection against the eavesdropping of information that is in transit in a communication system. However the benefits are not always easy to obtain. In many cases, the administrative costs associated with an encryption system can outweigh any benefits. Encryption techniques can be used to provide other useful services for an IT communications system; in particular, digital signatures, non–repudiation and anti–tamper checks. Encryption can solve some, but not all, communication security problems. For encryption to be at all effective it has to be combined with appropriate physical security measures and procedural measures.

5.3 The Kerberos Authentication Dialogue

The MIT Project Athena was a research project to implement a set of secure networking protocols. Many of the results of this project have been incorporated into present day networking. Microsoft are even providing a fairly complete implementation of Athena as part of the secure networking part of Windows 2000. The Kerberos dialogue is the mechanism which allows a user to authenticate himself to the system and to have allocated to him those resources to which he is entitled for the duration of a session.

This description is a slightly simplified version of the actual process. However it contains all the essential elements so that the reader should be able to understand how the dialogue maintains the security and integrity of the system. The aim of the dialogue is to ensure that password exchanges are achieved in a secure way and that system resources are restricted to those entitled to use them. The resource granting dialogues are conducted in such a way that almost no information as to what is going on can be gleaned by unauthorised listeners on the network.

In outline, the Kerberos authentication system works like this:

- There is a network of server hosts and client hosts. There are separate server hosts for all the main services: application server, file server, mail server, print server etc. In addition, there is an *authentication server* (sometimes known as the *ticket server*).
- The authentication server holds copies of all passwords: user passwords and server passwords.
- When a user wishes to use a service, he requests a "ticket" from the authentication server. This "ticket" can be presented to the service server to indicate that the user is entitled to use that service.
- To protect the authentication dialogues from eavesdropping, and to protect the system from a possible replay attack, all tickets are symmetrically encrypted with keys known to the recipient.

There are additional complications to handling the initial user logging in procedure. The client host and the authentication server have to exchange user name and password details securely using a process such as the Diffie–Hellman system.

The ticket is a small record with the following fields:

The session key: a private key shared only by the authentication server and the user client for the duration of the session. A copy of this key is passed to the client as part of the initial login authentication dialogue.

The ticket owner's username.

The client host network address: typically an IP address.

The service name: of the service for which permission to use is granted.

The time stamp: which indicates when the permission was granted and for how long the permission is valid.

The ticket is encrypted by the authentication server using the password of the service requested by the client. This means that the client does not get to know the password of the service provider nor can he read or tamper with the contents of the ticket.

When the client makes an actual service request, he sends a copy of the ticket together with his username and address encrypted using the session key. The server can decrypt the ticket, since it was originally encrypted using the server's own password. Once the ticket has been decrypted, the server knows the session key. It can then decrypt the username/address using the session key and check it against the details supplied in the ticket (which is, to all intents and purposes, tamper-proof). Provided everything checks out, the server will carry out the service.

The ticket contains a time stamp and a life span indicator so as to prevent anyone saving a copy of a ticket for later use. The life span of a ticket can be set for any period from a few seconds up to several days. In practice, the life spans of tickets are between two and eight hours. If a user remains logged in for an extended time, the authentication server will force the user to conduct a reauthentication dialogue once the initial authentication period has expired.

5.4 Hacking

A *hacker* is someone who attempts, and often succeeds, to gain entry into a computer system and browse. Frequently, a successful hacker will leave a *visiting card* behind to prove to the system's owner that he has been there. The majority of hackers are relatively harmless, and do no permanent damage. The worry associated with hackers is if someone can get into a system for fun then the system is vulnerable to the professional with unfriendly intentions.

How do hackers get in? Normally, hackers use the public telephone network to gain access to the system. Having got that far, the next problem is to login to the system. There are a number of ways of achieving this and they will vary from system to system. For example, in most interactive systems, the maintenance engineer will have an account with many of the privileges of the system manager. Further, for the convenience of the various casual engineers who come to the site to maintain the computer equipment, the password will be fairly simple or even standard. Once the hacker has logged in as an engineer he can browse sufficiently to find a friendly user account which he can adopt. Using the system privileges assigned to the engineers' account, the hacker can change the adopted user's password and assign to it sufficient privileges to enable him to continue his browsing unhindered. Some systems have weaknesses which enable the cognoscenti to bypass the login dialogue altogether!

Even if this form of attack fails, there are several other forms of attack. To illustrate the sort of technique used by hackers, take the approach generally adopted for an attack on a BSD Unix system. Generally, the attacker's first objective is to obtain *user* status on the target machine. Usually, the easiest way of achieving this is via a network connection. For computer networks to function in a user-friendly manner, one networked computer must be able to exchange administrative information with its logical neighbours. There are application programs which can exploit these facilities to gather information from the network and display it to the user. In the Unix world the following are frequently used:

rup: this program broadcasts an "all stations call" requesting all computers on the local network to reply with their identity and an indication of how busy they are. To a hacker, this amounts to an à *la carte* menu of machines to attack.

rwho, rusers: these programs lists users who are currently logged onto computers on the network. This provides the hacker with the names of valid user accounts on the network's computers.

finger: this program delivers quite detailed information about the user in question, including for how long the user has been logged in or, if the user is not currently active, when he (or she) was last logged in.

In these circumstances, a typical hacker will mount an attack using his own computer attached to the network he proposes to attack. The great advantage of such an approach is that he can set up user accounts with known passwords, at will, on this machine to assist in the attack.

The next layer of weakness is that, generally for convenience and occasionally to enable certain types of legitimate network administration, a computer may be set up with a list of other computers that it may "trust". Trust here means that someone may login to the computer in question from any computer in the trusted list without having to submit a password. The files in question are /.rhosts and /etc/hosts.equiv. Unfortunately, Unix systems are distributed with these files allowing all other computers to be considered, by default, to be trusted!

Armed with a list of likely computers and another list of valid user names, the hacker can set up pseudo-accounts for these users on his own computer.

Thus there is a strong chance that the hacker can login to a valid user account on one of the target computers by attempting to `rlogin` onto a selected target computer using one of the newly created pseudo-accounts.

Once logged onto a target machine, the hacker starts the second stage of his attack. This phase usually consists of identifying a suitable unused, or little used, account from which to exploit his penetration of the system's defences. To do this, the hacker needs to assume *superuser* (known on different systems variously as *root, system,* etc.) privileges and set the password to something he knows.

It may be thought that the assumption of *superuser* might be almost impossible for the normal unprivileged user. Unix, and similar systems, have a number of commands which need *superuser* privilege to execute. Such commands are marked with special bits in their control information which enables them to execute with the privileges associated with their owners. Examples of such programs in a Unix system are `passwd`, `lpr` and `sendmail`, all owned by *root*. When these programs execute normally, they are quite safe. However, when they execute abnormally (under certain error conditions) they can be persuaded to use their privilege to perform some act which results in the invoker having *superuser* privileges assigned to them. Whenever a way of exploiting a weakness in one of these programs is found, the program in question will need to be amended to eliminate the weakness. This is usually implemented in the form of an emergency "patch" which has to suffice until the next full upgrade to the operating system.

The primary defence against hacking is to avoid any direct connection with the public telephone network if at all possible. If such a restriction is impractical, then there are a number of possible ways to minimise the risks from hackers:

- The operating system should be kept up-to-date with all the latest authorised security "patches". Generally, these are issued to eliminate security vulnerabilities as soon as possible after they are found.
- All system files should be set up with the correct ownerships and access permissions. With very few exceptions, none of the system files and directories should allow normal users to write to them.
- *Superusers* should never execute files which can be written to (altered) by any normal user. To reduce the risk of a *superuser* inadvertently executing an untrustworthy file, he should obtain that status either by logging in directly as `root` or using the "su -" command rather than the simple `su` version.
- If the computer system supports the facility, the boot password mechanism should be implemented to prevent any unauthorised person rebooting the system into *single user mode* which would allow him to gain *superuser* privileges without the use of a password. Ideally, all *server* computers should be kept under secure conditions so as to reduce the risk to a minimum.

- The network configuration files /.rhosts and /etc/hosts.equiv should be empty (if possible), but should never contain a line consisting of "+:".
- The computer system should be connected to the public network via an answer back modem. This device does not permit a caller from the network to make a direct connection to the computer system. Once the caller has identified himself to the modem, the modem clears down the call then dials the caller using a predetermined number.
- The computer system can be connected to the public network via a manual switchboard. The switchboard operator must authenticate the outside user before connecting him to the computer.
- Finally, go through the checklist at the end of Chapter 6.

The next line of defence is to enforce a procedure which ensures that user s are chosen randomly and are changed on a regular basis. This is especially true for users who have any system privileges associated with them. Ideally, passwords should be generated by a suitable algorithm which generates random "words" (which do not appear in a dictionary). The computer system should store user passwords in encrypted form only in a file which is inaccessible to normal users. The normal encryption method used is a modified form of the DES algorithm.

As an additional precaution, it is considered good practice for a computer system to ignore a terminal for a period of five seconds or so after a failed login attempt. This is to defeat any attempt by one computer trying to crack a password in a target computer using an exhaustive trial. If all failed login attempts are logged and an alarm is raised as soon as the number of failed attempts exceeds three then there is some hope of tracing and catching the hacker.

There is no complete defence from the determined hacker. However it should not be too difficult, nor too expensive, to make life quite difficult for him. The main lines of defence are to avoid direct connections to public communications networks, and to implement a sensible password policy. What makes life difficult for a hacker cannot be assumed to be a complete defence against the determined professional snooper.

5.5 Unix and the TCP/IP Family of Protocols

The first conscious attempt to design and implement a rugged and flexible transport layer protocol was the DARPA-sponsored Transmission Control Protocol (TCP) for ARPANet. The original ARPANet transport layer protocol assumed perfect protocol layers beneath it and was generally unsuited for the hostile environment of defense data communications. TCP was finally completed in 1979. Whilst it provided all the services that one might expect of a transport layer, the cost was a very large header.

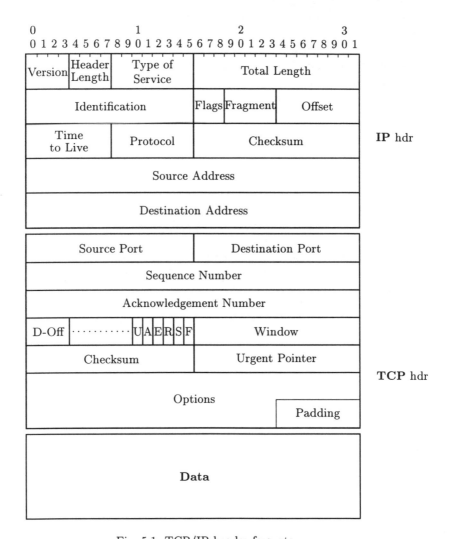

Fig. 5.1: TCP/IP header formats

The function of TCP is to enable a "message" to be split up into convenient chunks (packets) for transmission over a digital communications network, and for the "message" to be accurately reconstituted from the component packets at the destination. TCP makes no assumptions as to which order the packets arrive at the destination; the various fields in the TCP header contain sufficient information for the packets to be assembled in the correct order.

TCP also allows for a number of simultaneous logical connections between a pair of stations. Each logical connection is identified by a *port number*. The TCP header provides for a different port number for each direction. In the Internet, there is a convention that certain port numbers are reserved for specific services. For example, port number 80 is assigned to HTML (Internet browser) services. A list of some of the port numbers assigned to the more common services is given in Table 5.1. The security significance of port numbers is that they can be checked by *firewall* systems (see the next section) to determine whether a packet should be accepted or rejected.

Table 5.1: Some common internet services and their port numbers

Service	Port Number
FTP	21
Telnet	23
SMTP	25
Ping	79
HTTP	80
NNTP	119

The format of the TCP header is given in Figure 5.1. The important features of TCP are:

- the ability to check whether a packet came from the expected address and was delivered to the correct addressee;
- a high level of confidence in the detection of all duplicated and missing packets across resets at the transport protocol level and all lower protocol levels;
- the ability to reassemble a message and correctly sequence it from fragmented packets caused by limitations in other parts of the network;
- the provision of a multiplexing service;
- the provision of a number of differing levels of service.

The Internet Protocol (IP) is a relatively simple protocol whose main purpose is to ensure that a packet of data is passed safely across the network. The protocol is closely based on the IMP-IMP protocol and assumes the use of TCP for the transport layer. The IP protocol bits comprise a binary "envelope" around the data section which will include the TCP header together with the fragment of user data. The IP header is shown diagramatically in Figure 5.1. The most significant fields in the IP header are the source and destination address fields. The whole of the header is protected by the sumcheck field.

The TCP/IP protocols are not very secure. They perform their communications transport very reliably; however, there is no attempt to check that each packet actually came from the network address in the header. Since it is a protocol designed to allow packets to get to their destination by any route in no particular order, it is relatively easy for a hacker to insert a forged packet into the network. Such a rogue packet will have little effect on the communications but may have a disastrous effect on the application using the communications.

5.6 Firewalls and Gateways

One approach to reducing the risk of hacking is the use of a *firewall* system between a wide area network and a local area network to be protected from hackers. A firewall is a collection of simple computer systems whose purpose is to block unwanted protocol packets (a *packet filter*) and to hide the structure and internal addresses of the local area network from the wide area network (a *bastion host*).

A packet filter works on the principle that for an outsider (on the wide area network) to be able to set up a service connection it must send a service initiation (request) packet to a specific port on the host that is to supply the service. If the policy is that a particular service is to be denied to outsiders then the packet filter is set up to block any such service request packets from the wide area network. This is achieved by the filter host inspecting all the incoming packets; in particular, the destination host and the destination port are checked against permit tables configured by the system manager. The permit tables also specify the action to be taken by the filter host. Such action can be one of the following:

- allow the packet to pass through to the output port unchanged;
- change the destination address before passing the packet to the output port;
- change the destination port before passing the packet to the output port;
- change both the destination address and the destination port before passing the packet to the output port; or
- completely block the progress of the packet.

Should the filter encounter a packet of a type not listed in the permit table, then the filter host will take a predetermined action which can be any one of these, usually the last option.

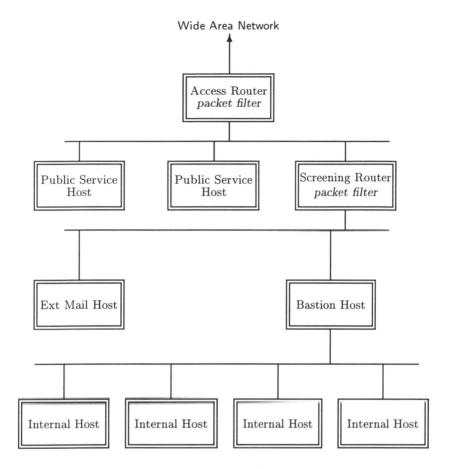

Fig. 5.2: A typical firewall configuration

A full Internet service is quite complex and involves several different protocols, several different destination (server) addresses and many different port addresses. The correct configuration of a single filter host to provide a complete and correct service is extremely difficult. In particular, a minor adjustment to the filtering function of one service may produce side effects which affect the configurations of other services. Consequently, the preferred approach to the defence of a private local network from an attack from the Internet is to split the filtering function between a number of filter hosts arranged in layers as shown in Figure 5.2.

The second function of the firewall is to hide the structure of the local network from the world outside. This is achieved by the bastion hosts which act as proxy servers. For example, an e-mail bastion (proxy) host assumes the identity of the e-mail address host. It will also have an address table which is used to determine the actual destination address from the addressee's name.

The structure of a typical firewall system is shown in Figure 5.2. In Figure 5.2 the *access router* is the first line of defence in the firewall. Its function is to block unwanted packets from the wide area network. The *screening router* is the second line of defence; its function is to prevent IP address spoofing and to ensure the only connection to the wide area network is from the bastion host (see below). It also prevents attacks on the internal local area network being mounted from any of the possibly subverted public service hosts.

A bastion host is the only host visible to users on the wide area network and thus it hides the structure, and even the existence, of the protected local area network. It accepts all incoming packets and, providing that they do not conflict with the local security policy, forwards them to the appropriate host on the protected local area network. For the maximum effectiveness, the bastion host should be configured with the minimum of functionality. There are two good reasons for this. Firstly, by eliminating functionality, there are fewer targets for a hacker to attack and therefore fewer risks of it being subverted. Secondly, if the bastion host is to check all the packets passing through it with the minumum effect on overall system performance, it is not a good idea to encumber it with functions best carried out elsewhere in the system. As far as the local area network hosts are concerned, the bastion host acts as the router to the wide area network.

Public service hosts supply services to users accessing the system from the wide area network. Typically, the type of services supplied by such a host are anonymous FTP and World-Wide-Web. It is prudent to use a separate host for each service so as to avoid the possibility of providing an (unintended) back door into the system by the use of another service.

The design of any firewall system should be determined by the following principles:

1. The firewall system should be as simple as possible consistent with the aims of the system. Simplicity is required so as to minimise the skill levels required to implement, maintain and use it.
2. Each of the protective modules of the firewall system should have as little functionality as possible.
3. Each of the protective modules of the firewall system should have as little trust of the other protective modules as is possible; they should not place any trust in any non-protected modules.
4. No trust should be placed in any user from the wide area network; neither should it assume that such users cannot mount an attack from the local area network, having already successfully penetrated the system's defences.
5. Only the necessary minimum of services are to be provided across the firewall system; any service not specifically allowed should be prohibited.

6. The firewall system configuration parameters should be protected against modification by anyone other than the system security officer; all changes to the configuration should be logged for audit and should be subject to strict configuration management controls.

For a more complete discussion on firewalls, see [17] and [48].

All communication, both legitimate and unauthorised, between the wide area network and the local area network must pass through the firewall system. This communication will be carefully controlled and logged in an audit trail. Using a firewall configuration like that shown in Figure 5.2 it is possible to monitor and log all attempts to hack into the local area network even if it cannot guarantee to block all such attempts. Thus, despite its name, a firewall system is not a "fire-proof" wall at all but more like a filter system. Like any filter system, there is a statistcal risk that a small quantity of unwanted packets may get through the filter.

Simple firewall systems that are correctly configured are useful and effective. However they do require regular frequent expert maintenance. Their very effectiveness may well cause an attacker to try another form of attack, out of frustration. The most obvious of these is a *spam attack*: this form of attack consists of bombarding the firewall system with flood of traffic in the hope of overloading the firewall system and causing it to crash. This is a form of denial of service attack. The danger at this point is for the system administrator to improvise a temporary service between the local area network and the rest of the world. The hacker is hoping for just this to happen as it gives him the opportunity to accomplish what he wanted to do in the first instance.

The simplest function of a firewall system is to filter out packets from proscribed or misconfigured sources. There are several IP addresses which should never arrive at a firewall from the world outside. In particular, there are a number of IP addresses reserved for local area networks (private intranets). Any packet bearing such a source address has either leaked out onto the Internet through a misconfigured firewall or is a cover for some form of unwelcome network mischief. A second class of IP address which should be rejected is one purporting to belong to the local intranet on the wrong side of the firewall. There is a third class of IP address which should be proscribed; that is a locally compiled list of unwelcome (but otherwise legitimate) IP addresses such as well known porn sites. Such simple packet filtering will eliminate most of the problem traffic from the outside world.

As most firewalls are configured to handle electronic mail in both directions, the simplest way to attack a firewall system is by using a spam mail generator directed to known or guessed user accounts on the target system. Such an attack should be taken seriously. Here are some general guidelines to cut down the risk of a succesful attack from the outside world:

- Monitor the packet arrival rate so that an alarm is set off when the packet arrival rate exceeds some predetermined (safe) value. In particular, close attention should be paid to packets attempting to open service connections. Many forms of denial of service attack take the form of tying up target network resources by never completing service connections and disconnections.
- The outermost filter host should be configured to slow down packet arrival rates using flow control mechanisms built into the communications transport layer protocol (normally TCP).
- All the processors of the firewall system should be very conservatively sized so as to handle the desired packet rates very comfortably.
- Very generous areas of disc should be allocated for message queue buffers. Such disc space should be on a different disc drive, if possible – or at the very least, a different partition to those holding system software.
- A competent administrator should check the free buffer space and for "dead wood" regularly and frequently and should take immediate remedial action when anything is found amiss.
- A competent administrator should look out for unexplained growth in the used area of the file systems.

The actual design, configuration and implementation of a firewall system is beyond the scope of this book. If this is a particular concern, you should read [2] and [17] which explain in great detail the particular weaknesses of the various components of the networking mechanisms and a number of measures to reduce the vulnerabilities resulting from these weaknesses.

Firewalls cannot be set up and forgotten!

5.6.1 One Way Filters and Related Systems

When a local area network carries particularly sensitive data, it may be necessary to be even more restrictive in the way such a network can be connected to the outside world. There are two possible ways of making such a connection and keeping the risks down to a manageable level. The first of these is a *one way filter* and the second is the use of multi-level secure software to police the passage of packets between the sensitive local area network and the outside world.

The one way filter approach is, in effect, a filter host configured so that only certain protocol packets may pass through the host in both directions and certain types of packet, in particular data packets, should be only allowed to pass from the world at large into the local area network and not in the reverse direction.

The use of a filter host with multi-level secure software relies on the fact that all data has to be tagged with sensitivity labels (systems certified F4 or DoD level B2 or above). The filter software can be configured to restrict the data passed out to the world to data with low sensitivity labels.

These two approaches have an important disadvantage. Whereas good firewall software is readily available, the same cannot be said for one way filters or multi-level secure software.

5.7 Communications Software Security Problems

The communications programs running inside computers usually have more privileges than normal users: they require these privileges so that they can control the communication lines and perform services on behalf of several users. For example, an e–mail utility needs the privilege to write an incoming message into the recipient's mail folder. Unfortunately, unless the communications software is fully debugged and every care has been taken in the design of the software to limit the scope of these privileges, it is possible for a remote user to cause such software to perform unauthorised operations which can undermine the security of the computer system itself. For more detail on this particular topic the reader is referred to Chapter 6 and [2] and [6] on the security problems associated with TCP/IP and Unix communications.

Most of the Unix communications software derives from the BSD sources; consequently, any weakness found in one Unix dialect is quite likely to manifest itself in most other dialects. One generic security weakness with these programs is related to the way the program stack is managed. The problem is that there is no check on the size of the buffer being read into the program. There are a number of attacks which exploit this particular weakness. The general method of attack is to construct an attack message which overflows the message buffer in the stack. The data in the message is such that the return address from the message read procedure is overwritten so as to force a return to another procedure which executes the supplied parameter string (also embedded in the attack message). The embedded command is executed with *superuser* privileges; the attacker can choose any command he (or she) wants to side-step the Unix protection mechanisms.

This weakness is not quite as bad as might appear at first sight. Firstly, it is widely known about and understood. It is also quite simple to cure: replace the old versions of the software with the latest versions. The actual programs which manifest this problem are mostly the communication *daemons* e.g., inetd, ftpd and telnetd. In general, versions with revision dates later than 1996 no longer manifest this problem.

The second "strength" (if that is the right word) is that the attacker has to know in advance the host architecture and the operating system version before an effective attack message can be constructed.

There is another form of attack used by hackers to obtain *superuser* privilege which exploits a weakness in the sendmail program. If this program is invoked with a delivery address macro whose expansion does not terminate, the program crashes leaving the user with a *superuser* prompt (#).

three morals one can derive from this section: firstly, ensure
latest version of the operating system software is used. Secondly,
unnecessary exposure to such forms of attack from external sources
use of firewalls or call-back modems. Finally, even if you have invoked
the best and latest precautions, it would be very rash to assume that
your installation is "hacker-proof"; all that you can assume is that you have
secured yourself against the currently known attacks.

5.8 Summary

The widespread networking of computer systems is a comparatively recent
phenomenon. Consequently, IT communications security is an area of much
current research effort. There are still a number of areas of current research
aimed at reducing the risks associated with data communications security
problems:

- the discovery of security holes in existing data communications systems
  and their plugging;
- the design of protocols which minimise the risk of spoof and replay attacks;
- firewall configurations which minimise the risk of unwanted accesses by
  outsiders at the same time minimising the restrictions to local users attempting to use wide area networks.

There are still a number of problem areas to be solved before computer
networks containing sensitive information can be directly connected to public
networks. In the meantime, the best advice is to minimise the number of network applications to the justifiable minimum, and to use properly configured
firewalls and vigilance.

Chapter 6

Unix Security

6.1 The Security Problems of Unix

The original design for Unix did not have security issues as a first priority. It was intended as an environment for the rapid and efficient development of software. Purely fortuitously, Unix had a number of features which could be adapted to provide some security. All the comments about Unix security weaknesses apply equally to Linux. As usually supplied, the Unix defaults effectively disable most of the obvious security features:

- The *superuser* account has no password.
- The networking configuration files effectively ensure that, by default, the host trusts all other hosts on the network.

As well as these basic weaknesses, it is possible to nullify all Unix's security defences by poor system configuration and bad administrator practices.

There are a number of notorious events which amply demonstrate that Unix is not impervious to attacks from outsiders. The most famous of these is the Internet Worm created by Robert T Morris and launched in November 1988 ([7], [35] and [37]). Clifford Stoll of the Lawrence Berkeley Laboratory spent nearly a year tracking a group of five German hackers ([40] and [41]). These hackers attempted to gain access to over 400 computer systems around the world and actually succeeded in gaining access to about 30. The hackers turned out to be working for the KGB. Other documented security problems include:

- Breaks into NASA's SPAN network [23];
- The IBM *Christmas Virus* [87];
- The virus at the Mitre Corporation that caused the MILNET (the US military version of what is now called the Internet) [11];
- The DEC-NET worm [12];

63

- Successful breaks into US banking networks [13].

These incidents have taught us about design weaknesses in systems which were previously thought to be impregnable. Unfortunately, not everyone seems to have taken the lessons from these incidents very seriously.

At the turn of the millennium, Unix based operating systems can claim at least 20 years of experience of combating security problems. There are two comparative newcomers: Microsoft's Windows NT and Linus Torvald's Linux.

Windows NT was designed and originally implemented by a team largely recruited by Microsoft from the Digital Equipment Corporation (DEC) VMS implementation team. Their brief would appear to have been to splice the Microsoft Windows friendly user interface with the functionality of VMS.

6.2 Unix File Permissions

The key to the security of a Unix installation is the correct setting of file access permissions. Almost any errors in the permissions of system files can result in security weaknesses. The general principles behind the correct settings for system file permissions are listed in the guidelines below:

- No directory in the superuser's PATH should have *world write* access. Similarly, no file in such a directory should have *world write* access.
- Only designated executable files should have `setuid` or `setgid` permissions.
- World writable files and directories are a security risk and should be eliminated as far as possible. The exceptions to this rule are:
  - `tmp` directories;
  - certain device files in the `/dev` directory.

Appendix A lists packages which contain shell scripts which can be used to scan the system for some of the more obvious weaknesses.

6.3 Executing as the Superuser

The `superuser` or `root` is a very special user who has the power to override all the Unix protection features. The superuser is necessary for some occasional but essential administrative operations, for example:

- installing or upgrading the system;
- altering the system configuration (e.g., adding a new printer);
- creating and deleting user accounts;
- backing up users' files;

- mounting and unmounting file systems.

However, it is not a good idea for the superuser to perform ordinary transactions for a number of reasons:

- A mistaken command would be executed overriding all protections. The worst sort of error is something like "`rm -rf ./*`" executed in the wrong directory.
- The wrong instance of an overloaded (ambiguous) command can be executed inadvertently.
- Under certain circumstances, a hacking attacker can take over control of an executing user.

Unnecessary execution of commands by the superuser exposes the system to needless risk. This risk is increased by the superuser executing certain commands, in particular, mail clients and Internet browsers. To reduce this risk to the essential minimum, the following rules are recommended:

- Where practical, disconnect the machine from the network to perform superuser administrative functions;
- The superuser "PATH" variable should be very restricted: e.g.
    `PATH=/usr/bin:/usr/sbin:/bin:/sbin`
- The superuser path should never include the current directory ("."). It is not advisable for the superuser path to include application directories such as "`/usr/local/bin`".
- Only the superuser should have write access to any directory in the superuser's "PATH".

6.4 Password Security

6.4.1 Selecting Passwords

The object when choosing a password is to make it as difficult as possible for an attacker to second-guess what you've chosen. This will force him to perform a brute force search, trying every possible character – letters, numbers, punctuation and control characters. A search of this sort on a computer, assuming that it could try 100,000 passwords per second (e.g., a 1GHz PC), would require, on average, over one thousand years to complete. Given such a specification for a password, we need to comply with the following guidelines:

- **Don't** use your login name in any form (as-is, reversed, capitalised, doubled, etc.).
- **Don't** use your own name, or any part of it, or that of your partner or any other near relation – in fact, names in general are not a good idea.

- **Don't** use other information easily obtained about you. This includes license plate numbers, telephone numbers, national insurance numbers, the make of your car, your house name, etc.
- **Don't** use a password of all digits, or all the same letter. This significantly decreases the search time for an attacker.
- **Don't** use a word contained in (English or foreign language) dictionaries, spelling lists, or other word lists.
- **Do** choose a password that is at least six characters long.
- **Do** choose a password containing both upper and lower case letters; upper case letters should be in the middle of the password rather than at the start.
- **Do** choose a password with non-alphabetic characters, i.e., digits or punctuation, for example "3-peNce".
- **Do** choose a password that is easy to remember, so you don't have to write it down.
- **Do** choose a password that you can type quickly, without having to look at the keyboard. This makes it harder for someone to steal your password by watching over your shoulder.

Although this list may seem to restrict passwords to an extreme, there are several methods for choosing secure, easy-to-remember passwords that do follow these rules. Some of these include the following:

- Choose a line or two from a song or poem, and use the first letter of each word, for example, "In Xanadu did Kubla Kahn a stately pleasure dome decree" becomes "IXdKKaspdd".
- Alternate between one consonant and one or two vowels, up to eight characters. This provides nonsense words that are usually pronounceable, and thus easily remembered: for example "routboo" or "quadpop".
- Choose two short words joined by a punctuation character, for example: "dog;rain", "book+mug" or "kid?goat".

As the number of users of a system increases, it becomes more difficult to ensure that all users choose good passwords. Unfortunately, it only needs one user to choose a soft password to provide a relatively simple way in for an attacker. To counter this, the more secure systems do not allow users to choose their own passwords at all. Such systems use password generators which automatically choose good passwords.

The importance of these password selection guidelines cannot be overemphasised. The Morris Internet worm, as part of its strategy for breaking into new machines, attempted to crack user passwords. First, the worm tried the obvious such as the login name, user's first and last names, and any other information gleaned from the password file. Next, the worm tried, in turn, the words held in an internal dictionary of 432 words (presumably Morris considered these words to be good words to try). If all else failed, the worm tried going through the system dictionary, /usr/dict/words [37]. It has been estimated that this attack strategy enabled Morris to break into nearly 30% of all user accounts attempted. The password selection guidelines proposed here have been chosen so as to defeat almost any password attack based on Morris's attack strategy.

6.4.2 Password Policies

Although asking users to select strong passwords will help improve security, by itself this is not enough. It is also important to form a set of password policies that all users must obey, in order to ensure that an attacker cannot effect an entry into the system through the exploitation of weak passwords.

First and foremost, it is important to impress on users the need to keep their passwords in their minds only. Passwords should never be written down on desk blotters, calendars, and the like. Further, storing passwords in files on the computer must be prohibited. In either case, by writing the password down on a piece of paper or storing it in a file, the security of the user's account is totally dependent on the security of the paper or file, which is usually less than the security offered by the password encryption software.

A second important policy is that users must never give out their passwords to others. Many times, a user feels that it is easier to give someone else his password in order to copy a file, rather than to set up the permissions on the file so that it can be copied. Unfortunately, by giving out the password to another person, the user is placing his trust in this other person not to distribute the password further, write it down, and so on.

Finally, it is important to establish a policy that users must change their passwords from time to time, say twice a year. This is difficult to enforce on Unix, since, in most implementations, a password-expiration scheme is not available. However, there are ways to implement this policy, either by using third-party software or by sending a memo to the users requesting that they change their passwords.

This set of policies should be printed and distributed to all current users of the system. It should also be given to all new users when they receive their accounts. The policy usually carries more weight if you can get it signed by the most "impressive" person in your organisation (e.g., the president of the company).

6.4.3 Checking Password Security

The procedures and policies described in the previous sections, when properly implemented, will greatly reduce the chances of an attacker breaking into your system via a stolen account. However, as with all security measures, the system administrator must check periodically to be sure that the policies and procedures are being adhered to. One of the unfortunate truisms of password security is that, "left to their own ways, some people will still use cute doggy names as passwords" [18].

The best way to check the security of the passwords on your system is to use a password-cracking program much like a real cracker would use. If you succeed in cracking any passwords, those passwords should be changed immediately. There are a few freely available password cracking programs distributed via various source archive sites; these are described in more detail in Appendix A.

6.4.4 Password Ageing

Many sites, particularly those with a large number of users, typically have several old accounts lying around whose owners have since left the organisation. These accounts are a major security hole: not only can they be broken into if the password is insecure, but because nobody is using the account anymore, it is unlikely that a break-in will be noticed.

The simplest way to prevent unused accounts from accumulating is to place an expiry date on every account. Such a mechanism is simple to implement. Account expiry dates can be held in the password file (or the shadow password file). A shell script is run daily to check accounts that have passed their expiry dates. When an account expires, it is rendered inaccessible to all users and a message is sent to the system administrator so that appropriate action can be taken. These expiry dates should be near enough into the future that old accounts can be deleted in a timely manner, yet far enough into the future to avoid enraging current users. Just before the account is due to expire, the user should be sent a warning e-mail so that the user can perform a simple action which results in the account expiry date being put back for a further period. A sensible figure for the expiry period is between three months and one year.

6.4.5 Guest Accounts

Guest accounts are a security breach waiting to happen. The problem is that these are fully functional accounts hanging around, rarely used, just waiting for attackers to practice unnoticed. To make matters worse, such accounts are, all too frequently, set up with rather obvious passwords such as "guest" or "visitor". The recommended approach to cater for occasional users is to have a shell script which will set up a new account when it is required and another shell script which will remove the account as soon as it is no longer needed.

6.4.6 Accounts Without Passwords

Some Unix system installations include a number of special accounts with such names as "lpq", "date", "who", "sync", "shutdown" etc. The purpose of such accounts is to allow normal users to execute privileged commands without having to know the superuser password. They work by virtue of the /etc/passwd entry for these pseudo-users having the command to be executed in place of the user login shell. These accounts have no password and are usually pseudonyms for "root". Consequently, such accounts are gifts for attackers to exploit. Such are the risks associated with them, all such pseudo accounts should be removed from the "/etc/passwd" file.

6.4.7 Group Accounts and Groups

A group account is a single account shared by several users, usually collaborators in a project. Such a set-up involves several people sharing a single password which is not a secure thing to do. The correct way to set up a project with several collaborators is as follows:

- An account, with a password and a home directory, should be set up for each collaborator in the normal way.
- Set up a *group* for the project. The members of the group should be the list of collaborators. This is achieved by adding a line in the "/etc/groups" file which is something like:
  proj_name:*:12345:collab1,collab2,collab3,collab4
  where "proj_name" is the name for the group, the "*" is the unused group password field, "12345" is the groupid, a number in the range 0 to 65535, and the last field consists of a comma separated list of group members.
- Any files which belong to the project should be associated with the group "proj_name" and have appropriate group read/write permissions. The group affiliations can be set up using the "chgrp" command and the permissions set up with the "chmod" command.

The Unix group system allows a user to be a member of several groups. Consequently an individual collaborator can participate in any number of projects. By following these guidelines, the functionality of group accounts can be implemented without any of the security risks associated with shared passwords.

6.5 Improving Unix Network Security

Unix systems can be configured to be fairly secure. However, the process is far from trivial. Most Unix distributions come configured with minimal security. The "friendly" default configuration is to ensure that group working can be implemented with the minimum of effort. Such a default configuration is relatively easy to hack into. Worse still, once an attacker has established himself on one of the hosts, it requires very little effort to establish himself on any host he chooses.

A second problem with older versions of Unix is a buggy communications library which affects nearly every TCP/IP related utility. The problem is related to the *buffer overflow attack* (see Section 5.7). Most Unix distributors can supply a debugged version of the offending library together with debugged version of the TCP/IP utility binaries. This latter step requires the system manager to be aware of the problem and to ask for the safe version of the software.

6.5.1 Trusted Hosts

One of the more convenient Unix networking features is the concept of "trusted hosts". This feature allows a particular host to nominate other hosts, or particular users from other hosts, who can use some of the resources of this host without the inconvenience of having to type a password.

This feature is reasonably safe when used in small isolated networks. In larger networks there are a number of potential problems. The most serious problem is the default configuration to treat every other host as "trusted". This means that someone logged in as the superuser on any machine can access any other Machine with superuser privileges without any restrictions.

The next problem is that Host A can be configured to trust Hosts B, C and D. Host B can, in turn, trust Hosts E and F, and so on. The problem here is that a user on Host F can gain access to Host A via Host B. Unless the configuration files which control the spread of trust are very strictly controlled, it is frequently possible for someone logged onto any host on the network to gain access to any other host on the network without the use of a password.

This situation is a hackers' paradise.

The remainder of this section is a summary of the vulnerabilities of the most common applications using the Internet. The discussion is based on the model shown in Figure 6.1 in which there is reference to a *Firewall System*. Firewall systems are discussed in Section 5.6 above. The assumptions made in this model are that users out on the Internet cannot be trusted at all but local LAN users can be supervised and given some level of trust. This may be a little naive since insiders are responsible for most recorded hacking attacks. Hence the use of this model implies that it must be complemented by sensible personnel security measures.

Unless otherwise indicated, the LAN hosts are assumed to be using a variant of Unix; towards the end of this section, there is a short discussion on the equivalent vulnerabilities of Windows NT. If you need to delve deeper into this topic, you are recommended to refer to the book "Maximum Internet Security: A Hacker's Guide" by Net Sams [32].

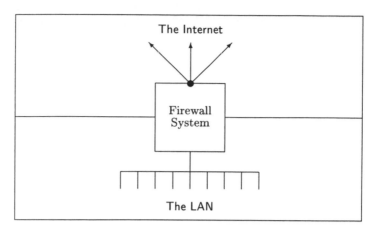

Fig. 6.1: The firewall system model

6.5.2 The r*xx* Utilities

There are security holes in all of the Unix r*xx* utilities, particularly rlogin, rcp, etc. These utilities are implemented using trusted daemons which contain bugs. These bugs can allow remote users to obtain superuser privileges without having to give a superuser password. To avoid this vulnerability, such utilities should not be available to non–local users at all and should be implemented for local users only if there is no suitable alternative. As well as these restrictions, all files which propagate remote login privileges (/etc/hosts.equiv, /.rhosts and ˜/.rhosts) should be deleted.

6.5.3 The finger Utility

The finger utility allows a remote user to obtain user account information from a host or a server. This is not a great problem in itself, however, it does give a hacker useful information (in particular, a list of user accounts to attack plus the identity of the operating system which may open up other possible lines of attack). The finger utility requires the services of a fingerd daemon; this daemon could contain holes. The presence of this utility is more a threat than an asset. It should be disabled: the system start-up scripts should not load the fingerd daemon.

6.5.4 The telnet Utility

telnet is a relatively safe alternative to rlogin. Even so, there are some risks associated with it. Some versions of telnet inadvertently give away security information: it gives a different response to different login errors. When the user name does not exist the dialogue is terminated immediately; if the user exists but the password is incorrect, then the user is allowed further attempts to repeat the login dialogue. The real threat from the `telnet` program is that it is possible (optionally) to specify a particular port number in the destination host rather than the standard `telnet` port number (23). This is a useful communications debugging tool but it can be abused and is the basis of quite a number of remote attacks.

In the right hands, `telnet` is an innocent enough facility. Because of the risks associated with `telnet` abuses, it is not recommended to allow the use of `telnet` from outside the local area network.

6.5.5 The `ftp` Utility

`ftp` is only as safe as the way it is configured. As well as the risks associated with incorrectly configured systems, so versions of the `ftpd` daemon have bugs which can supply unauthorised users with login shells, in the worst cases with **superuser** privileges. In some systems, a hacker making a `telnet` connection to port 21 (the `ftp` port) and issuing the `ftp` command "SITE EXEC" may be furnished with a shell. Despite these problems, it is usually safe to allow users to use `ftp` within the LAN; but it is not recommended that outsiders should be able to use `ftp` through the firewall system.

There is an `ftp` facility known as **anonymous** `ftp` in which outsiders can access a server using the pseudo user **anonymous**. This can be particularly risky. If a site wishes to have an **anonymous** `ftp` server then, as well as ensuring that it is configured properly, this server should be dedicated to providing this service. In particular, the **anonymous** `ftp` server should not host other functions such as `http` or `e-mail` as these functions have been known to interact with `ftp` in a way which increases the vulnerabilities. The `ftp` server host should be one of the *public service hosts* indicated in Figure 5.2 below.

It is also advisable to ensure that there are no writable directories on the `ftp` server. If a hacker can load a hostile executable onto the host then there is a likelihood that he can either execute the executable directly or trick `ftp` to execute it on his behalf with disastrous results.

6.5.6 The `tftp` Utility

`tftp` is essentially a very much stripped down and simplified version of `ftp` with no checks whatsoever. This utility was designed to allow the booting of discless workstations across a network. As a protocol it is extremely insecure, indeed dangerous. It is highly undesirable to attempt, even, to boot a computer across the Internet. Consequently, there should be no requirement to use the `tftp` protocol across the Internet. There should also be no requirement ever to use `tftp` over a LAN unless there are discless workstations on the LAN. It is very strongly recommended that the tftpd daemon should be removed from every host on the LAN and that the firewall system should be configured to exclude tftp packets altogether.

6.5.7 The http Utility

The http protocol are used by web browsers and therefore must be the most widely used application protocol on the Internet. There are no real problems with the http system as such, it is the misuses of the system which are the threat. The biggest threat is if the httpd daemon is run with superuser privileges: this would give outsiders browsing the server site superuser privileges with possible disastrous results.

If a public http service is to be provided then there should be a host dedicated to this function. The http server host should be one of the *public service hosts* indicated in Figure 5.2 below.

6.5.8 The nfs Utility

The Network File System (nfs) is administratively very convenient but there are vulnerabilities if the nfs subsystem is incorrectly configured. There are reports of vulnerabilities whereby hackers exploit nfs weaknesses to gain unauthorised access to local system resources. There is a tool called nfsbug available from the Internet

  (ftp://ftp.cs.vu.nl/pub/leendert/nfsbug.shar)

which scans your system for known nfs configuration vulnerabilities and reports those which it finds.

nfs is sufficiently useful for it to be implemented within the LAN. If this is done then the LAN must be protected by a firewall system configured to block access to ports 111 and 2049 from the outside world.

6.5.9 E−mail

Perhaps the second most widely used Internet service is electronic mail. It is unfortunate, then, that standard e−mail utilities such as sendmail and pop have vulnerabilities. sendmail is a very flexible program with a plethora of security holes. The most dangerous holes allow an unauthorised user to execute commands with superuser privileges. The very worst hole, corrected in the latest releases, allowed a local user to obtain a shell with full superuser privileges. Because of these problems, responsible management are effectively presented with a stark choice: either a properly configured and maintained firewall system and Internet e−mail or no Internet e−mail facilities. The firewall system should be checked regularly and fairly frequently to deal with *spam attacks*, i.e., a denial of service attack consisting of bombarding the target site with huge volumes of e–mail. There is a danger that a *spam at-tack* could cause the firewall file system holding the mail spool directory to overflow or the file system holding the firewall system log to overflow. Either occurrence will cause the firewall system to grind to a halt or, in extreme cases, crash thus making the attack successful. Hence the necessity to service the firewall system frequently.

6.5.10 The X Windows System

The X windows system is a flexible mechanism which allows a program to execute on one machine (the client) and to display its results (and to be controlled) from a second machine (the server). All that is needed is a com-munications channel between the two machines. When the client machine and the server machine are the same machine, there is no problem. When the two machines are different, then the server machine has to enable the client machine. This is achieved by the execution of the command xhost +*server–machine–name*. The greatest risk is that the command xhost + is executed which would then allow any machine on the network to control the client machine.

There are two risks with X windows: firstly, that an X server can be subverted by a hostile host and, secondly, the dialogue between an X client and an X server can be hijacked by a hacker (a *switch* attack). Even so-called secure X implementations are not very secure. It is strongly recommended that any X windows network activity should be confined to a LAN protected from attacks from the Internet by a suitable firewall system (see next section).

6.5.11 Windows NT

Despite the fact that this is supposed to be a chapter discussing the secu-rity holes in Unix systems, a word or two should be said about Microsoft's Windows NT operating system. Microsoft have ambitions for Windows NT to take over the large server market from Unix.

Like Unix, Microsoft Windows NT has a proper security model which works well provided that it is configured properly. For this security model to have a chance, the Windows NT system should be installed on NTFS file systems rather than FAT file systems. NT's access control mechanisms do not work on FAT file systems; the access control mechanism is essential to prevent unauthorised users changing user privileges and access rights by modifying registry files. The discussion that follows refers to NT 4 rather that NT 3.51. The latter contained several known security holes; most of them have been addressed in NT 4.

Windows NT is very different in design to Unix. Consequently, NT is unlikely to have the same security problems as Unix. In particular, an NT workstation is configured to manage one user at a time (in contrast to Unix which is a true multi–user system). This means that NT does not need the concept of privileged daemons to handle communication services on behalf of an arbitrary number of users. Consequently, the Unix daemon vulnerabilities do not exist in NT.

Although there are significantly fewer reports of security holes in Windows NT 4 than those of Unix systems, this does not mean that NT 4 is any more secure than Unix. The main reason for the disparity in the number of reports is that Unix has been around and exposed to hackers for some 18 years or so compared to NT 4's four years.

It is known that networked NT is vulnerable to `telnet` attacks into particular port numbers. In particular, there are known problems with port numbers 80, 135 and 1031. There are published fixes for the first two of these but it is thought that port number 1031 is still vulnerable. There may be other "port holes" as yet undiscovered.

There are reports that the NT password mechanism is vulnerable to an attack in which a special "`dll`" file is implanted into the NT host; this software then scans the password file and outputs user names and passwords in clear.

Machines running Windows NT should be kept physically secure as a hacker with a Linux floppy boot kit (a floppy with a boot kernel plus a second, known as a "rescue" disc) can boot the machine up, mount the system NTFS partition and edit the registry files directly. There is also, in the wild, a commercially available DOS boot disc which has the ability to reset managers' and administrators' passwords.

Because of the marked differences in design between Unix systems and Windows NT systems, it is suggested that a Unix intranet should be protected from external attacks by a firewall based on Windows NT. Equally, a Microsoft based intranet, using Windows NT servers and clients running Windows NT or Windows 98, should be protected by a Unix based firewall. The main advantage of such an arrangement is the wide range of skills the hacker must bring to bear to get round both systems. The main disadvantage to the implementor is that it requires both Microsoft trained personnel and Unix trained personnel to administer such an arrangement.

Chapter 7

Internet Security

7.1 External Hazards

Even if you have a very secure computer system yourself, when you join the Internet there are more potential problems which can arise from the service provider which connects you to the Internet. These service providers are known as *Internet Service Providers* (ISPs).

For most people, the gateway to the Internet is through an ISP. The main exceptions to this generalisation are some medium-to-large businesses, universities, some government establishments and ISPs themselves. For the rest of us, it is convenient and economic to hand over all the hassle to an ISP. It would be nice to think that all ISPs act totally responsibly and protect their clients from all known security threats. Unfortunately, this is not always the case. This chapter covers the more important threats and some appropriate countermeasures.

Let us start by describing what a typical ISP might look like. In the simplest of cases, it will consist of a Unix computer (or a Windows NT computer) with a reasonable amount of disc and a multiplexer connecting the computer to a large number of serial land lines. Such a system would be adequate for a small business with minimal security concerns. A large ISP will have a minimum of two medium to large server computers each with multiple processors. These computers will be attached to a disc farm with RAID and backup facilities. Between the computers and the multiplexer, there will be a firewall system.

The first problem with ISPs arises from the very fast growth in the numbers of ISPs. Worldwide, the number of ISPs has grown from a handfull in 1992 to tens of thousands at the turn of the millennium. For an ISP to be set up and configured properly, there should be a system manager with computer system security expertise or a senior member of the ISP staff with security expertise. Some ISPs will have to do without such expertise since, in the short term, the world's universities and training establishments cannot

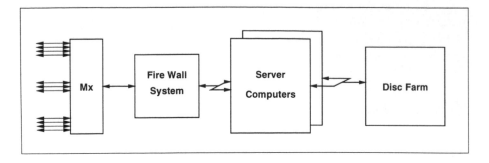

Fig. 7.1: An outline of an ISP installation.

keep up with the demand for highly-trained security experts from businesses, government departments and newly-emerging ISPs.

A logical consequence of this is that there are not many experienced ISP technical managers waiting around to assist in the setting up of a new ISP. Most ISP implementation teams learn on the job and probably make a number of errors early in the life of the ISP. If you are at all concerned with the security of your ISP, it is highly advisable to choose one that has been going for a year or two. By that time, they should have got over any teething problems.

There is a well-tried bit of wisdom for tourists in a strange town: choose a restaurant which is patronised by plenty of locals. This wisdom can be rephrased to "only use an ISP with plenty of subscribers". A successful ISP with a good number of clients is perhaps providing a good service and a good level of service (e.g., fast response times and a useful telephone help-line) to its user base. Magazine articles and reviews on ISPs should be treated with some suspicion. In most cases, the ISP would have gone out of its way to make a good impression to the reviewer and may not have been supplying a typical level of service. If you need help in the choice of an ISP, ask someone you know, and trust, for their opinion.

If an ISP has unwittingly misconfigured the computer system, it may be possible for hackers and worms to run riot throughout the ISP. For the clients, the threat is the possible loss of confidentiality and, in more severe cases, client data lodged with the ISP can be changed or even deleted. This scenario is far from being hypothetical: during the year 2000 at least one major UK bank, offering Internet banking services, has been embarrassed by the accidental disclosure of client bank account details to other clients.

Another embarrassment arose from the use of the Internet browser *back* button from a computer terminal in an Internet cafe. In this case, an innocent user used the terminal to access his Internet bank account. When he had completed his business he logged out of the bank account and left the terminal. Then a second user came to the same terminal. Presumably, for reasons of mischievous curiosity, he started by clicking on the browser *back* button and was surprised to find himself logged back into the bank account of the previous user without even having to type a password. In this latter case, either the bank's server was not configured to flush any information associated with a user from the system caches when the user logged out or the ISP kept a local cache of recently accessed pages for too long.

These two examples were publicised by the press. There must be several more examples which have been covered up. Nevertheless, these examples, which did not involve any skilled hacking attempt, demonstrate the importance of correct and meticulous configuration of an Internet server system.

7.2 ISP Services

ISPs can provide three types of service. However, it is unusual for an individual ISP to provide all three. These three service types are:

Shell **accounts:** these are the easiest and cheapest for an ISP to provide. The user is accessing a Unix *tied shell* interface over a serial line. The interaction is entirely text based.

IP connection accounts: in which the user is (usually) supplied with a temporary IP address and has a full Internet connection with the ISP

Server specific accounts: in which the user uses an ISP supplied program in his client machine which communicates with an ISP bespoke server program via a serial line. This approach is to simplify (dumb down) access to the Internet. It has been referred to as the "Disney" approach to the Internet.

Shell accounts are riddled with security problems. Fortunately, the facilities provided by such accounts are so primitive, fewer and fewer ISPs offer this facility. However, if your ISP does provide such a service, find another ISP quickly. The danger is from the threat of an attack on the ISP through a *shell* account.

IP connection accounts are the most common. In these cases, the user is given a temporary IP address at the start of an Internet session. The user then continues with a dialogue over a serial (usually telephone) line using either SLIP (**S**erial **L**ine **IP** **P**rotocol) or PPP (**P**oint-to-**P**oint **P**rotocol. PPP is gradually taking over from SLIP. PPP is more secure than SLIP and handles communication breaks more gracefully than SLIP. Provided that the ISP servers are sensibly configured, both PPP and SLIP are reasonably secure.

Server specific accounts, such as those supplied by AOL, are about as secure as IP connection accounts. The advantage of such accounts to the ISP is that there is no need for a pool of IP addresses for user access.

There are a number of recorded successful hacks into ISP sites. The more alert ISPs recognise the symptoms of an attack fairly rapidly, thus taking immediate steps to safeguard the service and client data and instituting measures to block off that particular mode of attack in the future.

7.3 After an Attack

Once an attack by a hacker has been detected, the ISP should perform several precautionary administrative procedures. One of these, under the appropriate circumstances, is to change client (user) passwords. This is where serious problems can arise. The user, finding that he can no longer login, telephones the ISP and asks what is going on. There are a number of recorded instances of ISP employees, under the stress of dealing with a crisis at the ISPs site, freely giving passwords to users over the telephone. In the worst cases, it would have been possible for hackers to phone in and obtain genuine user passwords.

Another sensible step by an ISP after an attack is to investigate how the attack was effected and to determine what steps need to be taken so as to ensure that a repeat of such an attack will not be successful. As part of such an investigation, there should be some consultation with a Computer Emergency Response Team (CERT). The original CERT was created in 1988 by the US Defense Advanced Research Projects Agency (DARPA) to address computer security concerns on the Internet. Since that time it has collected the details of all major security incidents on the Internet, has coordinated the reaction to these incidents and has formed the focus of the dissemination of good practices and remedies to specific security problems on the Internet.

Since 1988, most other nations with an interest in the Internet, have formed their own national CERTs. These CERTs keep in touch and cooperate with each other and with major industrial parties such as computer manufacturers, software developers and the major ISPs.

After a security incident, a good ISP should proceed with extreme caution. In particular, they should challenge the user so as to determine the identity of the caller before entertaining any dialogue about changed passwords. The same should apply when a user rings up about "forgotten" passwords or any other discussion concerning passwords. It is not a good idea to pass long-term passwords over the telephone, nor is it a good idea to share a password with an ISP employee. The preferred way to proceed is for the ISP to set up a one-time password (single use password) which is passed to the user. The user should then, without delay, login to his account and immediately choose a new (different) password.

The problem for the user is to determine if a particular ISP will respond in a responsible manner to an attack. In the best cases, the ISP should inform all users that a serious attack has taken place and that registered users should perform some sensible steps which should include changing any potentially compromised passwords and checking the user's files for anomolies. Should any anomolies be detected, then the ISP should be informed so that the ISP can restore any affected files from backups.

If the ISP admits to an attack but is adamant that their procedures are so perfect that they can assert that there is no need for users to take any action, then this should be the cause for user concern. Such an approach is taken out of ignorance or sheer arrogance. These organisations would seem to be more concerned with their perception of public confidence in themselves as an organisation rather than any concern for security.

The very worst ISPs are those who fail to do anything. The users find strange things happening to their files and their e-mail. When concerns are raised with the ISP, there seems to be the minimum of interest and the user is fobbed off with words to the effect of "It must be your fault; it is something that you did...". Under these circumstances, do not bother to stay around hoping for an investigation. Jump ship immediately, and find an alternative ISP without delay.

7.4 Summary

As a user, the choice of ISP is very important if you are at all concerned about security. For many people, the price of the services provided by the ISP would appear to be paramount. For those users who are going to rely heavily on the service provided by an ISP there is a checklist (in Table 7.1 below) which should assist in making a good choice. Do not choose the first ISP that impresses you; make sure that you have a reserve ISP (or two). You never know when you might need one.

Table 7.1: ISP Checklist

☐   Is the ISP well established? (Has it been running for at least 2 years?)

☐   Does the ISP have a large customer base?

☐   Does the ISP liaise with a CERT?

☐   Does the ISP not offer *shell* accounts?

Chapter 8

Radiation Security

"TEMPEST" is the government codeword for the unintentional radiation leakage of information from electronic equipment. Theoretically, such radiation leakage can occur from almost any equipment. In IT systems, the most likely leakage is from the Visual Display Unit (VDU) drive circuitry. This effect can be unintentionally enhanced by the video cable which connects the computer base unit to the VDU itself. The nature of the threat as far as sensitive information is concerned is that the picture on the VDU screen is broadcast and is picked up on a suitably modified television some distance away from the IT system in question.

The problem is not confined to VDU screens; there are similar, but less severe, problems with laptop LCD screens and impact printers. However, to get useful information from the stray radiation from such devices requires more sophisticated processing than passing the signal through domestic television receiver circuitry. There is even some radiation from the motherboard, however, it is very difficult to obtain copies of the data actually being processed. However, the nature of the radiation contains information about the type of processing taking place. In some circumstances, even this elementary information could be a security problem.

The dissemination of information is not confined to radio waves. It is just as likely that information from computer systems is picked up by domestic wiring (mains or telephone) and/or plumbing and conducted to other parts of the building. In extreme cases, it is possible to make a telephone call to the computer room and for information to be extracted from a distance of several hundred miles.

Thus, there are two problems: firstly, there is the choice of equipment to minimise the likelihood of unwanted radiation of sensitive information. Secondly, there is the matter of the layout of the equipment so as to reduce the risk of conducting sensitive information out of the confines of the computer room.

The problem is quite real as a number of television programmes have been able to demonstrate over the last ten years or so. As the performance of computer equipment has increased over the years, the problem has, if anything, got worse. In particular, the requirement for ever higher resolution VDU screens has raised the frequency and power of the radiation from the video drive circuits. So what can be done about it?

In general, radiation security measures come in four guises:

1. Enclosing electronic equipment in an electronic (Faraday) cage so as to prevent any electronic emissions escaping;
2. Where complete enclosure of the equipment is not practical (e.g., a cable or a public telephone exchange), the information within the equipment is suitably encrypted;
3. Using equipment specifically designed to minimise stray unintentional radiation; and
4. Laying out the equipment so as to minimise the risk of monitoring or interference.

Enclosing a computer inside a Faraday cage is inconvenient and very expensive. This is only done as a last resort where there is no other feasible method of suppressing unwanted stray radiation. There is still the problem of arranging how essential services, such as mains and air conditioning, are fed into the Faraday cage without allowing any radiation to leak out of the cage.

The protection of sensitive information by encrypting it inside the machine is not really much use as, for the information to be at all usable, it must be decrypted before it is displayed on the computer VDU.

The most practical solution to the problem is the use of IT equipment designed to minimise the radiation of information. The easiest approach is to use IT equipment specifically designed to prevent unintended interference to domestic television sets. Fortunately, both the USA and the Federal Republic of Germany has strictly enforced radiation laws. Consequently the use of equipment designed and produced specifically for use in the USA or the Federal Republic of Germany have to comply with Part 15 of the FCC rules for a Class B computing device or the DIN equivalent. The main difference between such equipment and certified "TEMPEST approved" equipment is the lack of a suitable signal filter between the mains lead and the power supply unit.

In the absence of equipment certified to be FCC compliant, the next best thing is to choose equipment enclosed in a metal or metal–lined case (as opposed to a plastic case) that has a screened cable connecting the machine to its VDU and a VDU casing which is also lined with a metallic screen. Such construction does not guarantee to eliminate the radiation problem, but is a prerequisite to the control of radiation from the system. Provided that the equipment has been constructed by one of the more reputable, international organisations (such as IBM, Dell, Compaq etc.), the radiation problem should be reduced to manageable proportions; the radiation should be confined to distances of 100 metres or so in the open, or tens of metres in steel framed buildings.

In extreme cases, i.e., where the sensitivity of the information is such that cost is no object in the reduction of the risk of information leakage, it is possible to purchase "TEMPEST approved" equipment from a number of defense suppliers. However, there are a number of disadvantages to the use of such equipment:

- The equipment will be relatively large and heavy compared to the latest equivalent domestic equipment;
- The technology used in the "TEMPEST approved" equipment will be, almost certainly, half a generation or more behind in technology, speed, reliability and power consumption compared to the latest equivalent domestic equipment; and
- The cost of such equipment will be at least twice the price and can be as much as ten times the price of the latest equivalent domestic equipment.

From this, it is reasonable to deduce that "TEMPEST approved" computer equipment should not be used unless the information it contains is of the most sensitive nature.

There is some threat of dangerous stray emissions from electronic equipments other than conventional desktop computers. Laptop computers contain similar video drive circuits to desktop machines, but without an external cable to connect it to the VDU screen. Even so, laptop machines do radiate. There are similar, but lesser risks from some printers and mice. With these latter devices, the snooper needs to know about the equipment under observation and has to do quite a lot of processing of the signals to get any useful information from the radiations of such equipment.

8.1 Equipment Layout

In most circumstances it is possible to avoid having to go to the extremes of purchasing "TEMPEST approved" equipment by sensible siting of a computer system containing sensitive information. The threat then becomes that of someone trying to monitor emissions from the organisation's IT equipment using UHF receivers in the back of a van parked in a nearby car park. In general, such a computer system should be kept separate from other systems, off the ground floor, and it should be sited as far as possible from public highways and particularly from vehicle parks.

It is not sufficient just to worry about emissions from computer cabinets and displays; one also has to consider signals leaking from the cabling connecting the various boxes. In any practical installation there will be other services such as telephones, mains electricity and even central heating. The design of the installation layout should aim to minimise the likelihood of cross talk from the computer system onto these other services. As a general guide, signal cables should not run near to, or parallel to, service cables and ducting. Where possible, they should be separated by at least 1 metre. Where they cross, they should do so at right angles.

8.2 Maintenance

It is all very well if new equipment does not inadvertantly radiate; it is equally important that the equipment still does not radiate after two or three years near the end of its useful life. In the most sensitive cases (in fact, ideally, in every case) the equipment should be resurveyed for radiation every 6 months or so and whenever the equipment enclosures are opened to maintain or upgrade the equipment.

8.3 Summary

The whole area of radiation security is a very large subject. In particular, the design of electronic equipment to minimise stray radiation is a very specialised subject in its own right. A full treatment of radiation security is beyond the scope of this general guide to information security. If more detailed information is required, you are advised to obtain the relevant Tempest publications listed at the back of "Computer Security Basics" by Russell and Gangemi [31].

With normal information, even commercially sensitive information, the risks do not warrant the full set of TEMPEST countermeasures. These are only required for the most sensitive information affecting national security. Reasonable levels of protection can be achieved by a combination of choice of site, sensible wiring layout and the use of equipment complying with the appropriate FCC rules.

Chapter 9

Procedural Security

Procedural security measures are those which do not come conveniently under any of the preceding headings. The most important security measure of all is that there should be someone from the organisation appointed to take responsibility for information security (the System Security Officer – SSO). The next most important security measure is for the SSO to draw up a security policy and to submit it to senior management for approval. The subject of security policies is discussed in greater detail in Appendix D.

For the most part, the other procedural security measures consist of manual procedures designed to complement technical security measures. Of the many possible procedural measures, only a few are considered here. They have been chosen because they are applicable to the majority of computer systems.

9.1 System Integrity

The first of these is *system backups*. At first sight this would seem to have little to do with computer security. However, if one of the main aims of the security plan is to maintain the integrity of the data in the system, and a certain level of service to the user, then system backups (or dumping) must form part of the security plan. Essentially, system backups consist of copying all the vital data and program files of a system so that, should the operational set become damaged (by fire, software error or gross user procedural error), then the files can be restored to their state at the time of the previous security dump. There are special techniques available to minimise the loss of user work resulting from a disaster - however, a discussion of these does not concern us here.

9.2 Magnetic Media

The second of these is in the handling of magnetic media (discs, floppies and magnetic tapes). A classified disc (or floppy or magnetic tape) is a classified document in the same way as any classified paper document and has to be accounted for as such. There is, however, a difference: a disc or a magnetic tape can hold ten to several thousand times the amount of information held in a bulging paper file[1]. Thus the loss of one of these items can be very serious indeed. There is one other problem: whereas one can talk of "deleting a file" or "scratching a tape" this is merely a logical operation; it does not physically remove the information from the disc or tape. Even actually overwriting the information does not completely remove all traces of the original information.

As a consequence of this, there is a general UK national security rule that states that once a disc or tape has been classified it may never be downgraded. This rule is always true for UK TOP SECRET and can only be relaxed under very stringent conditions for UK SECRET and UK CONFIDENTIAL. This rule can be extrapolated into general commercial terms along the lines that any magnetic media used to hold Confidential or more sensitive information should not be returned to a general user pool. When such magnetic media is no longer required, it should be destroyed rather than put out for normal waste disposal.

9.3 Denial of System Benefits to a Competitor

The third of these lies in the emergency destruction of a system when it is just about to fall into the hands of a competitor. This aspect is particularly relevant to a tactical military computer system. The hasty destruction of discs and magnetic tapes is far from straightforward. If a system contains extremely sensitive information on magnetic media then much careful thought has to be given to its emergency disposal. To guarantee the permanent destruction of the information one has to use either very high temperatures ($> 800°C$) or dissolve the iron oxide in an acid bath; it is not desirable to have to carry the ingredients necessary to carry out such procedures in tactical military vehicles nor is it wise to stock quantities of such materials in commercial premises near to the computer centre.

---

[1] The approximate capacity of a reasonably full manila file is about 1,000,000 characters (1 MByte), which is roughly the capacity of a floppy disc. (This book is about 0.5 MByte.) A standard 1/2 inch magnetic tape can hold about 40-80 MBytes, a 1/4 inch cartridge tape about 60-150 MBytes, a digital audio tape (DAT) 2-5 GBytes, an Exabyte tape 5-10 GBytes and Winchester (hard) discs range in size from 50 MBytes to 9 GBytes.

9.4 Disposal of Documents

When sensitive documents are no longer required, they need to be disposed of
in an appropriate manner. There is no point in keeping them as there is still
a risk that they could be accessed by some unauthorised person and there
is still the cost of protecting them. This section discusses some appropriate
ways of disposing of sensitive documents.

The recommended disposal method is determined by the document's type
and its sensitivity. For convenience, documents can be divided into two types,
paper and magnetic.

9.4.1 Paper Documents

In this context, paper documents include books, manila covered files, loose
papers, computer punched paper tape and computer punched cards. There
are two problems when attempting to dispose of paper documents:

- contrary to a widely held belief, bulk paper is very difficult to burn, and
- even when a sheet of paper has been burnt, it is often the case that the
  original writing or printing is still legible.

Thus if sensitive paper documents are to be disposed of by burning, they
should be fed into the fire a few pages at a time and the ashes should be
raked over thoroughly. The latter is to ensure that there are no large sections
of burnt paper that can still be read.

Unrestricted paper can be disposed of in the same way as any other
waste, by putting it in the dustbin. However, if there is any danger that
there is any more sensitive waste mixed in with the Unrestricted waste,
the whole batch of paper should be disposed of as if it were of the same
sensitivity as the most sensitive waste in the batch. This can be quite tedious
and costly. Consequently, it is a very good idea to segregate sensitive waste
from Unrestricted waste.

Paper that is deemed to be Private needs rather more care in its disposal.
It can be either burnt in the way described above or it can be shredded using
a good commercial shredder. In the case of shredding, the resulting strips of
paper should be no more than 2mm ($\frac{1}{10}$in) wide and should be longitudinally
at right angles to the lines of writing. With these precautions, it may still
be possible to reconstruct part of a document, but the cost of reconstruction
may be out of all proportion to any benefit to be gained from reading the
document.

The most sensitive paper documents require disposal procedures which
make it almost certain that such documents cannot be reconstructed. The
problem is increased because there are relatively few documents of such sensitivity. There are two ways which ensure that reconstruction is virtually
impossible:

- shred the documents longitudinally and then carefully burn the shred-dings; or
- shred the documents longitudinally and then, again, laterally resulting in paper fragments about 2mm × 2mm.

Although the latter method would appear, at first sight, to be the more straightforward, it requires a very powerful, wider than standard, shredder to be capable of coping with the second cut. If the volume of highly sensitive documents is not high, the first method would be the more economical.

It could be said that having a separate disposal procedure for the most sensitive documents could be a problem in its own right as it advertises the volume of the most sensitive document holdings. Some organisations use the same disposal procedure for all sensitive documents thereby hiding the distribution of documents between the various sensitivities.

9.4.2 Magnetic Documents

Magnetic documents come in a number of forms:

- floppy discs,
- magnetic tapes coming in several forms: open reel, QIC, DAT and Exabyte to name four of the most common forms; and
- Winchester (hard) discs.

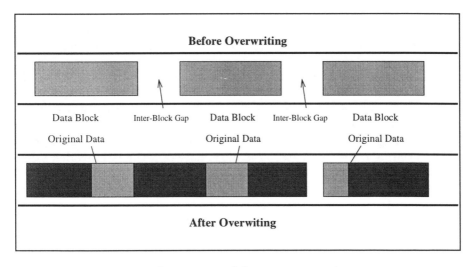

Fig. 9.1: Overwriting of data on a magnetic tape

It may be thought that it would be a quick and simple business to remove data from magnetic documents. Unfortunately, this is far from being the case. The "deletion" of a file from a magnetic document does not wipe the file from the document, it merely removes the entry for that file from the directory. The actual file itself remains until the space taken by the file is used for another purpose. To underline the point, many systems provide a utility to "undelete" the file – this merely reconstructs the directory entry for the "deleted" file.

Information is held on magnetic media using very small magnetic units arranged in long lines. This information can be destroyed in a number of ways:

- by carefully overwriting the original information with something else;
- by bulk erasure using a very strong electro-magnet which destroys the linear organisation of the magnetic domains, representing the original information;
- raising the temperature of the magnetic material to the "Curie" temperature (about 780°C for iron and 1000°C for Cobalt) thereby destroying the magnetic properties of the recording medium;
- physically destroying the magnetic documents.

Of these four methods of destruction, there are problems associated with the first two. Overwriting the original information in such a way as to guarantee that it cannot be reconstituted is virtually impossible. Nearly half of the information that has been "overwritten" once can be reconstituted with relatively little effort by a suitably determined individual.

Figure 9.1 shows how data is held physically on magnetic tapes. The data is in the form of blocks separated by gaps. For $\frac{1}{2}$ inch magnetic tape the data is written in 9 parallel tracks along the tape. Eight of the tracks hold user data; the ninth track holds lateral parity information. Thus a row across the tape holds one byte of data. The length of a block corresponds to the length of the data record written to the tape. Data blocks must be at least 12 bytes long and can be up to 65535 bytes in length. Typical records are between 80 and 4000 bytes long. Modern tapes can hold more than 10000 bits/inch, thus the length of a data block is usually between 0.008 inch and 0.4 inch long.

One of the more important features is the gap between individual blocks of data. This gap is known as the *inter–block gap*. This gap is required to allow for the mechanical acceleration and braking of the tape up to recording/playback speed and back to rest. For $\frac{1}{2}$ inch tape, the standard size for the inter–block gap is roughly $\frac{3}{4}$ inch; for QIC cartridge tapes, the gap is about 60mm. With modern flexible tape recording densities of over 250 bits/mm, there is scope for large amounts of data to survive in inter–block gaps.

Figure 9.1 shows a tape holding data long data blocks. The top line is before the original data is overwritten. The bottom line is after overwriting with different data. It shows that much of the original data may still be "visible" in the inter–block gaps of the newer data. In practice, provided the tape mechanism is functioning correctly, the situation is not quite as bad as

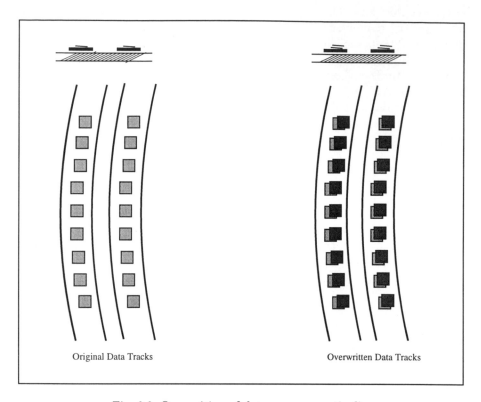

Original Data Tracks   Overwritten Data Tracks

Fig. 9.2: Overwriting of data on a magnetic disc

the diagram would indicate. The "bias" head should be switched on at least 0.1 inch before the start of the data block and should not be switched off until it is at least 0.1 inch beyond the end of the data block. Thus the effective gap between data blocks is about $\frac{1}{2}$ inch.

Figure 9.2 indicates how data is held on hard and floppy discs. The actual data is held in concentric rings known as *tracks*. Typically, a hard disc will consist of five aluminium plates with seven or eight recording surfaces. Each surface will hold over 1000 data tracks; in turn, each track will consist of about 80 data blocks each holding 512 bytes of data[2]. The actual data occupies a width which is about 40% of the distance between adjacent tracks. The effective width of the read heads is roughly one third of that of the write heads. Thus if an overwrite is not precisely aligned with the original data, it is possible to position the read heads over that part of the original data not overwritten by the new data. Hence the possibility of recovering much

---

[2] A standard HD floppy disc has a single mylar plate with two recording surfaces. Each surface holds 80 tracks each with 18 data blocks.

of the original data. There is at least one laboratory in the US which claims to be able to reconstitute some information after as many as 10 attempts at overwriting.

The problem with the second method is that it is almost impossible to produce a magnetic field strong enough to *guarantee* to obliterate all the data on the document outside of a well-equipped laboratory. (It is possible to produce such a magnetic field suitable to erase a floppy disc – however it is impossible to guarantee that the magnetic field has erased the whole of the disc.) Floppy discs are now so cheap – 3.5in High Density (HD – holding up to 1.44 MBytes) discs are about \$0.50 (30p) each in bulk – that it is not worth the risk of recycling them. The same argument can be applied to magnetic tapes. Winchester discs are rather more expensive, so the economics of disposal argument hardly applies.

9.4.2.1 Disc Partitions. Hard discs have one additional security problem. As indicated in Chapter 2, it is now the practice to divide hard discs into partitions. However, there is absolutely no guarantee that the area of the disc covered by all the partitions actually amounts to the whole disc.

There are in fact two mechanisms to create spaces in which to hide data on hard discs:

- The disc geometry (the number of cylinders, the number of heads and the number of sectors per track) as defined to the system software may not reflect the physical geometry of the disc — the most common is declaring fewer cylinders than the disc actually holds.
- Defining partitions which do not actually cover the whole disc, thus leaving bits of "unused" disc between partitions.

The security implications of this are as follows:

- Attempts to delete or overwrite any files on the disc, or ever to re–initialise (DOS format) a partition, will have no effect whatsoever on any data left in areas not covered by regular disc partitions.
- It is quite possible for someone trying to hide data to place it in areas of a disc not covered by the disc partitions. Such data might be of interest to investigators, particularly in fraud or pornography cases.

Without the requisite specialist knowledge, it is very difficult to detect rational attempts to disguise the disc geometry so as to hide data. This is yet another reason why attempts to wipe a disc by deleting or overwriting files using conventional commands cannot be guaranteed to be effective.

9.4.2.2 Dealing with Magnetic Documents. Because of the overwriting problems with magnetic documents there have to be restrictions on their reuse. Once a magnetic document has been used at a particular level of sensitivity, it should be treated as having at least that level of sensitivity for the rest of its existence. For example, once a floppy disc has contained

`Confidential` information, it should be treated as a `Confidential` document until it is finally destroyed.

Disposal of floppy discs is relatively straightforward. Both plastic and cardboard cased floppies can be destroyed in an incinerator. If no incinerator is available then the floppies can be cut up using a guillotine or a heavy duty shredder.

Magnetic tapes are slightly more difficult. The only guaranteed disposal mechanism is the incinerator. A tightly-wound mylar tape may not burn completely; but, the information will have been cleared because the tape will almost certainly have been raised above the Curie temperature.

The disposal of Winchester discs poses even more of a problem. The preferred disposal method is to attack the disc unit with a machine tool such a milling machine. They can be thrown into incinerators, however the molten aluminium of the casing and the discs themselves could ruin the incinerator. The author has succesfully used two methods of destroying sensitive hard discs. In both cases, the disc units have been mechanically dismantled so that the individual circular plates are separated from the rest of the drive. The drive casing and electronics were disposed of as normal waste. The plates were then either destroyed using a gas welding torch or placed into a trough of strong acid so as dissolve the iron oxide layer holding the information. (These procedures should not be undertaken lightly; in both cases, the processes are potentially very hazardous. They should only be carried out by suitably qualified personnel, wearing protective clothing in a suitable environment.)

9.5 Weeding and Downgrading

One very valuable and important piece of security advice is to minimise the amount of sensitive data to be protected. The normal use of a computer system containing sensitive information is going to result in a proliferation of classified files. This situation is exacerbated by the effects of the Bell and LaPadula model *-property[3]. To comply with this advice, system security officers and system should regularly check the file system for unwanted files or over-classified files.

To make the weeding task more manageable for the system administrators and security officers, users should be encouraged to carry out their own weeding on a regular basis. Where practical, the system administration should provide users with a straightforward mechanism to downgrade files. In most cases, it should be sufficient for the act of downgrading a file to be recorded in the system audit file.

---

[3] See Chapter 10

9.6 When It Starts to Go Wrong

Perhaps the most important security procedures are those designed to cope with situations where something has gone wrong. The generic name for such procedures is "recovery procedures". Any good organisation should try to predict the most likely disaster scenarios and formulate recovery procedures designed to restore a normal situation with the minimum of delay and effort. Having formulated a suitable recovery procedure, the staff should practise it regularly. This is important for two reasons:

- The staff need to know what to do in a crisis.
- Management have the opportunity to assess the effectiveness of the recovery procedure being practised and to make improvements.

It is not unknown for quite prestigious organisations to pay mere lip service to the practice of recovery procedures. For example, the last (and only) time that a full system fall back procedure was exercised was just before the system went live and operational. In the meantime, there have been two major operating system upgrades and only three staff members who were present at the original practice are still employees of the organisation!

So what can go wrong? And what recovery procedures should be drawn up? It is virtually impossible to predict all possible problems in all possible organisations. The actual situations which warrant specific recovery procedures should be determined by fairly senior management. There is a danger here of overkill: an attempt to draw up procedures for every conceivable crisis. Such an attitude can lead to an unnecessary waste of effort planning for disasters that are most unlikely to happen (for example, a severe earthquake in the Vale of York). The list of disasters below is intended to serve as an *aide memoire* rather than a check list for recovery procedures. Consideration should be given to drawing up recovery procedures from the relevant circumstances listed below.

- Fire in the computer suite (room).
- Natural disaster (flood, earthquake).
- Loss of electricity supply (power cut).
- Loss of environment control (e.g., air conditioning).
- Loss of local computing facilities (e.g., computer breakdown).
- Illness (absence) of a vital member of staff.
- Accident resulting in serious injury in the computer suite.
- Disc crash.
- Loss of internal communications (e.g., LAN).
- Loss of external communications.
- Loss of a sensitive document or magnetic media.
- Defection of a key member of staff to a commercial rival.

9.7 Summary

Procedural security is dominated by the safeguarding of dataa and the handling procedures for magnetic media and sensitive paperwork. Procedural security is made less costly and onerous if the amount of material to be protected is kept under control. Good procedural security consists of laying down sensible procedures, the carrying out of these procedures, and the audit mechanisms which ensure that the procedures are carried out effectively.

Chapter 10

Software Security

Software security is more difficult to achieve than it would appear at first sight. There are two facets to this:

1. firstly, there are the checks and procedures that can be implemented and enforced by software;
2. secondly, there is the testing and analysis of the programs to ensure that the checks are implemented correctly and completely. Further, one has to check that there are no other covert features anywhere in the programs within the computer system that would nullify any of the specified system defences.

Typical software security measures include:

Authentication: password checks upon logging in and even upon attempting to access or update certain important files.

Access control: checks by system software that particular users are permitted to access particular files or even certain fragments of information.

Labelling: enforcing the marking of documents printed by a computer with an appropriate security classification.

Accounting and audit: maintaining a record of all transactions which are relevant to security, e.g., changing the classification of a file.

Computer systems that are to be used to process, store or forward classified information should be accredited by the responsible Departmental Security Officer (DSO) to confirm that their use does not present an unacceptable risk to national security. In order to reach a decision on accreditation, the DSO will require an explicit statement from the manager of the computer system covering:

- the scope of the system;
- the nature of the security requirement;

- the specific measures that are to be implemented; and
- the allocation of responsibilities for enforcing them.

This statement, the basis for accreditation, is called a *System Security Policy* (SSP).

A computer system that is relied upon to enforce security measures is said to perform various *security functions*. Each security function can be considered to be a discrete aspect of the performance of the computer; however, in almost every case, its implementation will be interlinked with the implementation of other security functions of the developed system. When the computer system is to be relied upon to perform security functions, it is sensible to get a suitably qualified independent consultant to certify that the computer system meets the security requirement. In order to carry out the certification process, the consultant will need to be supplied with:

- a detailed statement of the technical aspects of the SSP (sometimes known as a *System Electronic Information Security Policy* (SEISP));
- the system design documentation of those parts of the system concerned with the enforcement of the security policy;
- in the most extreme cases, the source code of critical sections of code.

The purpose of the certification procedure is to ensure that the design correctly reflects the SEISP requirements, and the coding correctly implements the design.

The fundamental problem associated with all forms of software security is how one measures the effectiveness of the implementation against the original list of security requirements so that a suitably qualified security officer can assess the risks associated with entrusting security to the software. The mechanical analogue of this has been around for a long time: one gets an expert to assess the lock and construction of a safe so as to determine the risks associated with entrusting classified documents to its care. The expert looks at the specifications and drawings of the lock and the safe box and comes to some conclusions. In more critical cases, he will demand to have a sample safe so that he can physically test its capabilities. For the highest quality safes, each safe will have to undergo an individual security assessment. The latest software security assessment methods are analogous to the mechanical assessment methods just described.

Until the mid-70s, very few people had any notion how to carry out a software security assessment for computer systems. In the late 1970s the US National Security Agency (NSA) started to lay down the formal requirements for secure computer systems; these requirements are published in a number of documents known as the "Rainbow Books". The most significant of these was the Orange Book[1][26] and its Annexes. The first edition of the Orange Book

---

[1] The Orange Book is the colloquial name for the "Department of Defence Computer System Evaluation Criteria", Security Center, Fort George G. Meade,

appeared in 1983 and the latest (revised) edition was published in 1986. The purpose of the book was to list the required features of a computer system, to describe how those aspects were to be assessed for security purposes, and to list the criteria against which each aspect should be judged. (It does **not** lay down which criteria have to be satisfied for any particular circumstance, For US government agencies, these are defined in documents based on the *Yellow Book*. When a project manager is laying down the software security policy for a project, he is also strongly advised to get specific guidance from the appropriate security branch of the DoD.)

The Orange Book laid down some 27 properties of secure computer systems which required assessment and defined 7 levels of assurance. The list of security properties is very complete and includes such items as authentication, data access, event logging, security auditing and covert channels . As far as the UK security authorities are concerned, this list of properties constitutes a valuable checklist, however, not all computer systems require all the properties to be implemented to the same level of assurance. Indeed, in most cases, it would be highly uneconomic to attempt to do so. Consequently, the attitude of the UK authorities toward the Orange Book is as a guide to the spirit of good security practice but it should not necessarily be followed to the letter.

The most important aspect of the Orange Book lies in the definition of the 7 levels of security functionality together with associated levels of assurance. These assurance levels, in ascending order, are D, C1, C2, B1, B2, B3 and A1. Level D is reserved for those systems which have been evaluated but fail to meet the requirements of any higher level. Level C provides discretionary (need-to-know) protection, Level B provides Mandatory protection and Level A provides verified protection. A full list of the 27 security attributes and a full definition of the 7 levels of assurance are given in Appendix B to this book.

The second most important concept formalised in the Orange Book is that of the *TCB* (TCB). The TCB comprises the totality of security protection mechanisms within a computer system – including hardware, firmware and software – the combination of which is responsible for enforcing a security policy. It is recommended that the software part of the TCB, the trusted software, should be kept separate and independent from the rest of the system so as to simplify its design and verification. The ability of a TCB to enforce a security policy correctly depends solely on the mechanisms within the TCB and on the correct input of system parameters (e.g., a user's clearance) related to the security policy. All the levels of assurance, including C1 and above, assume the existence of a TCB which is capable of defending itself against attack from other parts of the system.

Maryland (DoD 5200.28-STD) Dec 1985 - The nickname arises from the book's orange colour.

10.1 Secure Computer Systems

There is a great demand within the defence community for a system which caters for several different classes of user, cleared to different classification levels (a multi-level secure system). The problem lies in producing software which can ensure that users cleared only to the lower classification levels cannot access any information at classifications greater than that for which they are cleared. Another problem consists of ensuring that a user cleared to a high level of classification cannot copy data from a highly classified file to a device fit only to handle lowly classified information (e.g., sending a SECRET printout to a printer in a public corridor). Fortunately it is not necessary to procure all computer systems to a specification which solves all these problems. When a computer system is being assessed for the risks it presents to the stated security requirements, it is convenient to categorise the operating mode into one of four possible modes:

Dedicated mode: in which all users are fully cleared to access all the data in the system and all users have a need-to-know for all the data,

System high mode: in which all users are fully cleared to access all the data in the system but do not necessarily have a need-to-know for all the data,

Compartmented mode: in which all users are fully cleared to access all the data in the system but do not necessarily belong to the specific (code-word) user communities for all the data; and

Multi-level mode: in which not all the users are cleared to access all the data in the system, and they usually do not have a need-to-know for all the data.

Dedicated mode places no reliance in the software to enforce any of the security policy but relies entirely on physical, personnel and procedural security measures. System high mode places some trust in the software to enforce the need-to-know principle but still relies on the other three classes of security measures to enforce the remainder of the security policy. Multi-level mode entrusts the software to enforce the majority of the security policy but still requires physical security measures to protect the trusted computer base (i.e. the computer itself and the associated discs etc.). Compartmented mode is a pragmatic compromise with nearly all the functionality of multi-level mode but with lower (less costly) levels of assurance. It is intended for use where all users are cleared to access all the data but segregation needs to be properly enforced between various user groups. As the trust in the software to enforce the security policy increases so does the required confidence level in the correct implementation of the software.

The differences between multi-level mode and compartmented mode are not particularly well marked, in practice, with respect to the detailed interpretation of the terms *clearance* and *need-to-know* with respect to differing levels of confidence in hardware and software. It is thus very difficult to draw up regulations which cover all circumstances. The recommended practice is to draw up specific requirements based on the SSP document for each project.

Since dedicated mode places no reliance whatsoever on the software to enforce the security policy, it is theoretically possible to use a DoD level D assurance (UKL0) computer system for this mode of operation. The trust placed in the software by a system high mode of operation requires the assurance level to rise to at least C2 (UKL2). The specifications for a multi-level secure computer system are relatively easy to generate. The difficult bit consists of producing the software to a level of confidence such that the danger of security breeches is kept to an acceptable level. The general rule for such systems is that provided that the highest classification of data on the system is SECRET then a system with DoD level B2 (UKL4) assurance is required. However, if the classification goes up to TOP SECRET then the required assurance level is A1 (UKL6). (This can be reduced to levels B2 and B3, respectively, (UKL4/5) provided all the users have udergone basic vetting procedures and that other physical and procedural safeguards are implemented as would normally be the case for an MoD system.)

10.2 Software Evaluation

The checking of software for correctness so that one can guarantee that it contains no errors (accidental or intended) is very difficult to achieve. Mere testing is insufficient; it is impossible to test exhaustively even the simplest of computer programs. To achieve the UK Assured Design Level of Confidence (UKL6), or the DoD A1 level of assurance, requires the use of formal evaluation techniques which use tools which are capable of determining from the documentation and the program source code that individual security requirements have in fact been implemented correctly.

One approach (still at the research stage in the US) is the checking of programs using automated theorem proving programs. This technique requires the "user" to lay down explicit formal requirements on the computer program, e.g., it should only calculate the gun lay and, furthermore, this shall be dependent only on the gun location, the target location, the ammunition and the meteorological data. There are two main snags to this approach: the first is that, even for very small programs (less than 50 lines of Pascal) this process takes a Cray–XMP2 supercomputer over 24 hours of computing to achieve; secondly, the theorem proving programs have yet to be formally proved themselves!

The method of the rigorous checking out of computer programs developed in the UK is known as Static Analysis (see Chapter 11). Very similar methods have been developed in parallel at Southampton University (SPADE) and at RSRE (now DERA), Malvern (MALPAS). Both SPADE and MALPAS consist of computer programs which analyse other computer programs. Each program of each suite is looking for particular aspects of the program under evaluation:

1. **The control flow analyser** checks the overall structure of the program under test. In particular, is there any part of the program which cannot be reached and is there a part of the program which has an entry point but no exit (a "black hole")?

2. **The data flow analyser** checks that all declared data variables are, in fact, used. It also checks that when variables are used, there has been a value already placed in the variable.

3. **The information flow analyser** checks that, for all the possible paths through the program, all variables have values assigned to them before they are used. Further, this analyser will produce a list of all variables for which data has to be supplied (inputs) and all variables which finish up with results in them (outputs) and, for each output, it lists all the inputs which contribute towards the value in that output.

4. **The semantic analyser** will generate the expression (or "formula") relating an output to its inputs.

Used by analysts with the appropriate skills these "tools" can indicate far more about a program than straightforward testing (dynamic analysis) can. The first two tools can be used as a general quality screening test of programs. More importantly, they are a necessary prerequisite for tools 3 and 4. The latter tools are very useful when checking a program for the presence or absence of particular features.

This type of formal analysis bestows other possible benefits on computer programs. In particular, static analysis frequently shows up errors (bugs) not discovered in the course of conventional testing. Although static analysis is quite expensive and time-consuming, the costs may well be recouped if it saves one panic re-issue of software to fix a serious bug discovered in the operational use of the programs.

10.3 Software Security Models

One is much more likely to place trust in a "secure" computer system if its design can be shown to conform to a recognised security model. These are discussed in a little more detail in Appendix C; of these, the most significant is the Bell and LaPadula model[1]. This model defines the required behaviour of the system in a precise and unambiguous manner. Given such a model, it should be a relatively simple matter to determine how closely the implementation conforms to the model definition.

The *Bell and LaPadula security model* is a formal specification of the most common governmental security policy. It can be summarised as follows:

- No *subject* (person or device) may access an *object* (information) the sensitivity of which is greater than the clearance of the subject.
- (Known as the **-property*) no subject may *write* to an object whose sensitivity is less than the clearance of the subject.

This policy specifies the relationships between system users and the information held by the system. The first part of the policy is what you might expect. It says *don't allow anyone to look at information for which they do not have clearance* and it should need little further explanation. The second part of the policy appears counter-intuitive at first sight and so deserves further explanation. What it says is that if a person creates or edits a document, the classification of that document must be at least as high as the clearance of that person. The logic behind this is that if a person has access to information up to classification $QQQQ$, then, potentially, material of classification $QQQQ$ may have been included in the document.

If a multi-level secure computer system based on the Bell and LaPadula security model has users cleared to classification $QQQQ$, then the **-property* will result in all the data in the system eventually being classified $QQQQ$. This is very inconvenient, so there must be suitable administrative procedures put in place to deal with this. The normal approach is to give each user several user identities or aliases, one for each working classification level between Unclassified and their clearance level. When a user logs onto the system, they have to choose the level at which they wish to work for that session and thereby select the appropriate alias. Once the user has logged onto the system, he will find that he can access all data classified at his login level and below but is denied access to any information classified higher than his login level. Any files created or edited will be classified at the login level.

The Bell and LaPadula model is insufficient to define the full behaviour of a secure system. There is still a requirement to define to whom a person may pass on information derived from the computer system: the system distribution policy. DARPA has recently sponsored work at MIT [2]; the Myers and Liskov model complements the Bell and LaPadula model and allows the "owner" of the information to apply restrictions on who may receive the information. Moreover, when information is derived from a number of independent sources, each source can specify its own distribution policy which contributes to the derived policy for the processed information.

10.4 Other Software Security Issues

Secure computer systems raise many philosophical problems. It is simple enough to state that user X can only access information up to UK

---

[2] **A Decentralized Model for Information Flow Control**, Myers A.C. and Liskov B., *Proceedings of the ACM SOSP 16*, October 1997: http://www.pmg.lcs.mit.edu/

CONFIDENTIAL. How does one implement the *aggregation rule* which states that the classification of a collection of data may be higher than the highest classification of any of its constituents? Modern technology raises another potential problem: it is now possible for certain system software to "steer" the read/write heads of a disc transport. (Normally, this facility is only available to the very highly privileged system software within an operating system which services the system discs.) Up until 1980 or so, it was accepted that under normal conditions, the act of overwriting data on a disc meant that the previous data was inaccessible unless the disc was subjected to certain laboratory information recovery techniques. The steerable head may allow any programmer to recover the previous data on the disc without it being taken off the machine! The practical multi-level secure computer system is still not available. It is expected that such systems may be available early in the next century. Advancing technology is assisting the researchers in some areas but it is complicating the whole problem in other areas.

Chapter 11

Some Notes on Static Analysis

(Much of the material of this chapter draws on Dr Bernard Carré's notes for his course on **Program Validation** *held at Southampton University in the Spring of 1983.)*

11.1 Introduction

This chapter is intended as a very brief introduction to program analysis. The examples of the techniques assume the use of the SPADE package developed at Southampton University by a team under Dr Bernard Carré. Firstly, a simple Ada example is introduced. This code is then subjected to analysis using the standard techniques of static analysis. The final section summarises the various strengths and weaknesses of static analysis.

11.1.1 Static Analysis

Static analysis is the technique whereby it is feasible, under certain conditions, to determine the properties of a program without actually running it. One can summarise static analysis under the following headings:

Control Flow Analysis (CFA): determines the overall structure of a program.

Data Flow Analysis (DFA): determines which routes through a program affect variables.

Information Flow Analysis (IFA): determines which *inputs* to a program affect particular *outputs*.

Semantic Analysis (SA): determines the resultant values in the program *outputs*.

105

Each of these techniques is discussed in turn below.

11.1.2 A Simple Example

Before we start on a detailed discussion of techniques, it would help if we were to introduce a trivial example so that we can illustrate what is being achieved. Let us solve a system of 2 simultaneous equations:

$$a_1 x + b_1 y + c_1 = 0$$

$$a_2 x + b_2 y + c_2 = 0$$

The following Ada fragment consists of a procedure, SOLVE, which, given the coefficients a1, b2, c1 and a2, b2, c2 delivers X and Y as the solution. To make the answer complete, the procedure also sets a BOOLEAN variable RES to indicate whether the values of x and y can be trusted.

```
procedure SOLVE (A1, B1, C1, A2, B2, C2 : in REAL;
         X, Y : out REAL;
         RES : out BOOLEAN) is

declare
      Q : REAL;

begin
         Q := A2 * B1 - A1 * B2;
         if ABS(Q /(A2 * B1 + A1 * B2)) > 0.0000003 then
            X := (B2 *C1 - B1 * C2) / Q;
            Y := (C2 *A1 - C1 * A2) / Q;
            RES := TRUE;
         else
            RES := FALSE;
         end if ;
end SOLVE;
```

11.2 Control Flow Analysis

CFA identifies all the possible paths through a program and the decision points within the program. It is a necessary prerequisite for all the following forms of analysis.

The result of CFA is to represent the program as an acyclic graph. The nodes of the graph represent the program *labels* and the arcs represent the actions. Note that the term *label* in this context is a little more general than the programmer's label; a labelled node is any point in a program where more than one execution path parts or meets. (It is rather unfortunate that the term label has a completely different meaning in the security domain, as defined in the Orange Book: a machine readable marking associated with an *object* (usually a file, record, field or document) defining the sensitivity of an *object*. This mathematical meaning of the term "label" should not be confused with with the meaning imposed on "label" bu the Orange Book.)

Figures 11.1 and 11.2 indicate how simple programming constructs are represented.

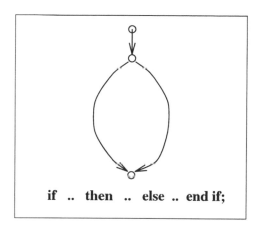

Fig. 11.1: The representation of a conditional statement

A Control Flow Graph (CFG) is a useful representation of a program in that it forms the basis for all further analysis of the program and any subsequent decision as to how the program should be recast for concurrency.

The CFG is useful for a second reason; it quickly allows the analyser to determine whether it will be possible to recast the program at all. The *forbidden* subgraph (see Figure 11.4) consists of a "loop" with more than one entry point. If this construct is detected, analysis (and even compilation) should be abandoned – with strongly-worded diagnostic messages! In a program containing this construct, it is impossible to produce an adequate definition of the concept of a "loop".

Other seemingly difficult constructs, such as multiple exits from "loops", can be redrafted as a *Dijkstra* structured program. This is indicated in Figure 11.3.

The algorithm which classifies the program structure consists of repeatedly applying the reductions indicated in Figure 11.5. Ideally, we should finish up with a graph consisting of a simple straight line connecting the start node

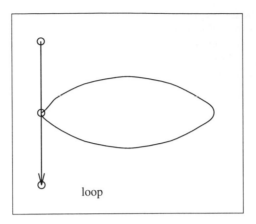

Fig. 11.2: The representation of a loop statement

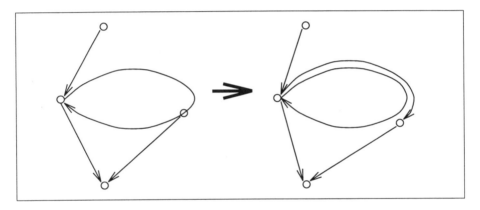

Fig. 11.3: Showing how a loop with more than one exit can be recast as a loop with only one exit.

and the end node. Such a program is said to be *Dijkstra–structured* or a *while–program*. If this is not the case, the program either contains the forbidden subgraph or it has more than one start and/or end node[1]. In either case it is unacceptable for further analysis.

In CFA there is the concept of *dominance*. If we have a control flow graph with a start node s and two other nodes x and y, the node x is said to *dominate* the node y if every path from s to y contains x. This relationship is be represented by the notation: x δ y.

---

[1] A "program" with more than one end node can arise from a procedure with more than one exit (**return**) statement.

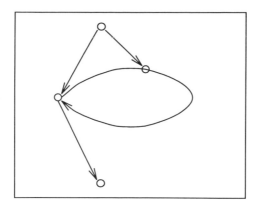

Fig. 11.4: The "forbidden subgraph".

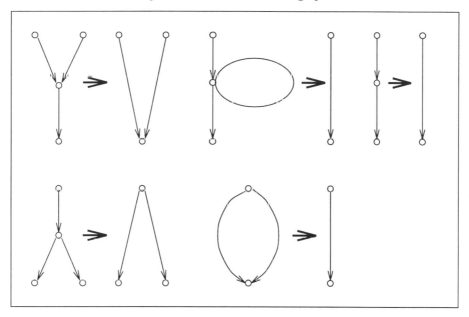

Fig. 11.5: Showing the reductions applied to a CFG to classify its structure.

The dominance relation has a number of properties:

- δ is *reflexive*: x δ x, for all x.
- δ is *antisymmetric*: if x $\neq$ y and x δ y, then y *cannot* δ x.
- δ is *transitive*: if x δ y and y δ z, then x δ z.

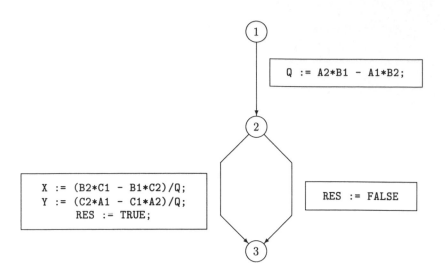

Fig. 11.6: The CFG for the example program

In our trivial example, the CFG consists of an arc followed by a pair of parallel arcs representing the alternative paths through the conditional statement. This is a "well structured" program, relatively simple to analyse as it does not contain loops with multiple entry points or multiple exits.

11.3 Data Flow Analysis

DFA is a useful prerequisite to IFA. DFA determines what data items are read and written to in each arc of the CFG. It is used by (good) conventional compilers as follows:

1. It can determine whether there exists a path from the start of a program to any point at which a data element is read before a value has been assigned to it. If none of the paths, between the program start point to the point at which a data element is read, include an assignment to that data element, there is said to be an *unconditional data-flow error*. If only some of all the possible paths do not assign values to the data element, the data-flow error is said to be *conditional*.

2. It can determine the life span of (static) variables within a program. From this information, some (FORTRAN) compilers optimise the use of storage by overlaying several variables onto the same storage space.

Program analysers use DFA to detect certain programming anomalies:

1. **The use of undefined variables** (as defined immediately above).
   Anomalies of this kind are serious coding defects. It is important that all
   such anomalies are found and rectified.
2. **Unused definitions**. A definition can be *unused* in one of two possible
   ways: firstly, a definition is said to be unused if, from the point of definition, there is no path to the end of the program which makes use of that
   definition; secondly, a definition is redundant if there is no use made of
   the defined variable before it is redefined. Such an anomaly may, or may
   not, be serious. It is good practice to investigate all such anomalies as, although they may be harmless, most arise from minor coding errors. Even
   if the program runs correctly, the redundant code makes the program
   unnecessarily complex and that much more difficult to maintain.
3. **Invariant definitions** and **tests**. A definition is said to be invariant if
   the RHS of the assignment consists only of constants and variables which
   are invariant. A variable defined thus is said to be a *masked constant*. Such
   a definition is not a serious anomaly; in fact, such definitions are found
   frequently in system software. However, invariant definitions found in
   loops can signal a problem, if only the unnecessary consumption of CPU
   effort. A test which consists only of constants and masked constants is
   more serious: usually it is invariant due to a coding error. Even if it is
   not an error, the arm of the test which is never executed could usefully
   be eliminated to simplify the program.

11.4 Information Flow Analysis

IFA is a logical extension of DFA. The first step of IFA is to construct for each
arc of the CFG the *inputs* and the *outputs* of the arc. For each arc *output*,
there is a list of *inputs*. By summing the *inputs* and *outputs* of each arc
across the whole or part of the CFG, it is possible to identify the information
dependencies within parts or the whole of a program.

In the analysis of programs, IFA is used to detect ineffective statements.
The designer of a program is expected to know what the program *outputs*
should be. A statement is said to be ineffective if it assigns a value to a data
element which is not an *input* to a program *output*. Some optimising compilers
detect such statements and discard them with a warning diagnostic message.

Program testers use IFA in a slightly different manner. They carefully
inspect the list of *inputs* for each program *output* for anomalies – unused
inputs, missing elements in the lists of *inputs* or unexpected elements in the
lists of *inputs*.

Again, in our trivial example, it can be seen that the outputs, x and y,
are both dependent on all the coefficients and the `result` returned by the
procedure is dependent only on the coefficients of x and y. If this were not
to be the case, there would be an error in the program.

$$x = f_x(a_1, b_1, c_1, a_2, b_2, c_2)$$

$$y = f_y(a_1, b_1, c_1, a_2, b_2, c_2)$$

$$result = f(a_1, b_1, a_2, b_2)$$

In the list of *inputs* which determine the resulting value of an *output*, there are two classes of variable. The first, and most obvious, consists of those which appear on the right-hand side of assignment statements which contribute to the final result. The second consists of those variables which appear in the Boolean comparisons which determine the actual path through the program used to compute a particular instance of a final result. The second class is called the *predicates*. In our simple example, a_1, a_2, b_1 and b_2 are *predicates* and a_1, a_2, b_1, b_2, c_1 and c_2 are all used on the right-hand side of assignment statements for both x and y.

11.5 Semantic Analysis

SA is the "ultimate weapon" in the analysts' tool chest. SA derives the actual algebraic expression for selected *outputs*, program or arc. SA carried out over a whole program is a slow and time-consuming process. However, it is possible to apply SA over short partial programs at not too great a cost in time. (SA has a running time proportional to the product of the number of possible paths through the program and the number of variables used).

SA is normally used on partial programs. A combination of CFA, DFA and IFA is used to identify that part of the program which affects the variable(s) of particular interest. The selected partial program is extracted and the (semantic) analysis is carried out on the partial program.

The results listed below indicate the kind of output one would expect from the semantic analysis of the procedure SOLVE.

$$x = \textbf{if } (a_2 b_1 - a_1 b_2)/(a_2 b_1 + a_1 b_2) > 0.0000003$$

$$\textbf{then } (b_2 c_1 - b_1 c_2)/(a_2 b_1 - a_1 b_2)$$

$$\textbf{else unset}$$

$$y = \textbf{if } (c_2 a_1 - c_1 a_2)/(a_2 b_1 + a_1 b_2) > 0.0000003$$

$$\textbf{then } (b_2 c_1 - b_1 c_2)/(a_2 b_1 - a_1 b_2)$$

$$\textbf{else unset}$$

$$result = \textbf{if } (a_2 b_1 - a_1 b_2)/(a_2 b_1 + a_1 b_2) > 0.0000003$$

$$\textbf{then TRUE else FALSE}$$

11.6 The Use of Static Analysis

Static analysis is a technique which is sometimes specified as part of the quality assurance procedures for high integrity software. The static analysis of software requires the software to be designed with this technique in mind, if the maximum benefit is to be derived from it. Consequently, if static analysis is mandated as part of the quality assurance, the specification of the software should be done in terms of assertions which can be proved (or disproved) by static analysis. For example, in a software system it would be reasonable to specify:

> There should not exist a path from the quiescent loaded state of the system to the user application state which does not pass through the user authentication module.

In more technical terms, the node representing the valid exit from the authentication module should *dominate* the node representing the start of the user application code. Expressed in such terms, this assertion should be verifiable from CFA alone.

The recommended approach can be summarised as follows:

1. Extract all the critical security (or safety) requirements from the system specification. Before progressing to the next stage, these should be agreed with the `Accreditation Authority`. In the case of the security requirements, these should be listed in the SSP document.
2. The critical security (or safety) requirements need to be recast into *assertions* which can be proved, tested or demonstrated. It is at this stage that those *assertions* which are to be "proved" by static analysis are identified.
3. The *assertions* need to be independently verified that they are equivalent to the security (*or* safety) requirements.
4. For each *assertion*, a test is specified so as to determine the compliance (or otherwise) of the final system. Where funds are limited, each test should be costed. Then, with the approval of the *Accreditation Authority*, the tests are prioritised. Before proceeding to the next stage, an agreement has to be made with the *Evaluation Authority* that the selected tests demonstrate compliance with the security policy.
5. Once the system becomes available for testing and analysis, the required tests are carried out and documented. Minor failures should be documented, rectified and retested.
6. The test results are submitted to the *Evaluation Authority* who make recommendations to the *Accreditation Authority*.
7. The *Accreditation Authority*, in turn, decides whether it is safe to bring the system into service and if there are to be restrictions on the use of the system or procedural work–arounds to compensate for any weaknesses discovered in the testing/analysis phase.

11.7 Summary

Static analysis allows us to determine certain properties without having to run the program. Whereas dynamic testing can tell us about the behaviour of a program for a (small finite) set of test data inputs, it can only indicate, by a possibly fallacious process of interpolation, how the program might behave for other intermediate data inputs.

It is very inefficient to attempt to use static analysis techniques to "fish" for unspecific design or software errors. The main purpose of such techniques is to provide answers to very specific questions about the behaviour of the software being analysed. These techniques are by no means a complete answer to a software tester's prayer. There are two main reasons for this: firstly, it is a fairly costly technique to apply – typically, the cost of analysis is about 20–30% of the cost of the generation of the software in the first place; secondly, static analysis can only answer a restricted number of questions about a program. In particular, it cannot normally tell us if the software actually computes the arithmetically correct answer to a problem – it only tells us how the software calculates the answer. As a technique, it should not be used in isolation but in conjunction with the traditional dynamic testing techniques.

Chapter 12

Computer Viruses

12.1 Introduction

Computer viruses are another class of security problem. They can be classed as such since, at the very least, they reduce the performance and availability of computer systems. They also consume valuable skilled manpower resources in their prevention and cure. Some of the more vicious viruses may destroy data or even render the system unusable. They are not a problem that can be ignored.

As the name for the phenomenon implies, a computer virus can be passed from computer to computer, or from program to program, without the user being aware of the disease until some unpleasant symptoms have manifested themselves. Computer viruses are contagious in that for a computer to become infected one of three possible conditions must exist:

1. the computer must be in direct communications contact with an infected machine; or
2. the computer must have read an exchangeable floppy disc (or magnetic tape) which was written to by an infected machine, or
3. the computer must have been directly infected by the programmer who created the virus.

In a computer network, if one of the machines is infected with a virus then all other machines on the network are vulnerable. Because files can be copied across the network, infected files can carry parasitic viruses with them. So far, there have been no recorded infections through the mains electricity supply.

The formal definition of a virus is:

a program that can "infect" other programs by modifying them to include a possibly evolved copy of itself.

115

As well as virus programs, there are a number of related types of program which are frequently confused with viruses. The first of these is a program which can propagate itself using communications facilities; these are usually known as *worms*. Such programs tend to replicate themselves in a very similar fashion to viruses so, for the purposes of this book, they will be treated as a special case of virus.

The next type of program which disrupts computer systems is a *Trojan Horse*. Such programs do, or pretend to do, something useful and, at the same time, they perform some unwanted action. The most obvious of these is the login Trojan Horse which presents the unsuspecting user with an interface identical to the genuine operating system login interface. The user is invited to login and to provide his (or her) password in the normal way. Having digested the user name and password (writing them away to a file somewhere) it responds with, for example, "logins are currently disabled, please try again later". This enables a crooked user to obtain unauthorised copies of various innocent users' passwords for some later use.

Trojan Horse programs can disguise themselves in the most ingenious of ways: perhaps the most insidious is the ANSI.SYS program which is the mechanism which configures the screen and the keyboard of a PC in to something resembling a traditional alphanumeric terminal. One of the features is that it allows the user to redefine the characters generated by each individual key of the keyboard. For example, the "\" key could be reprogrammed to generate the character sequence: "DEL *.EXE<*ret*>\". This would result in all the ".EXE" files in the current directory being deleted without the user being aware of what he had done or how it was achieved.

There are many other possible uses of Trojan Horse programs; almost all of them pose a threat to the security of a computer system. However, such programs do not, in general, attempt to replicate themselves and so they cannot be classed as virus programs.

A third type of threatening program is known as a *logic bomb* (or *sleeper*). A logic bomb is planted in a system where it lies dormant until the occurrence of a specific event or the coincidence of a number of circumstances. When the *trigger* occurs, the logic bomb is activated and performs its *payload* process, which may be benign, such as wishing someone a happy birthday, or it may be malicious, for example, deleting all the files in the user's home directory. Normally, logic bombs do not attempt to replicate themselves so they cannot be classed as virus programs. However, it is possible for a virus program to have a payload process consisting of a logic bomb.

A fourth class of threat is associated with Internet browsers such as Netscape and Microsoft's Internet Explorer. The actual threat is caused by Java and Active--X. Java is a portable interpreted programming language system originally from Sun Microsystems. Java programs can be imported into a browser from across the Internet and executed locally, typically to provide some special effect such as an animated picture. Unfortunately, the functionality of Java is not restricted to the implementation of special visual effects; it is a fully functional programming language whose programs can perform any operation limited only by the constraints imposed by the local environment. The problem is that a user can import an apparently innocuous program which has a covert side effect which may be any of the following:

- the import of a virus program;
- the alteration or destruction of some local files; or
- the export to a third party of information which may be used to facilitate a hacking attack (e.g., a copy of the local password file).

Active–X is a Microsoft proprietary product based on similar principles to Java but more oriented to OLE.

A fifth related threat is the so-called "Millennium Bug". This software problem is a legacy from the days when the 21st century was considered too far into the future to be worth considering. There are a number of variants of the problem; they all amount to the fact that, sooner or later, the storage space allocated to hold the current date/time value will overflow:

The "Millennium Bug" In many systems, dates are held in the form of six characters: DDMMYY where DD is the day of the month, MM is the number of the month and YY is the last two digits of the year. The problem arises that for the year 2000, the YY field has the value "00" which is less than "99" which represents the value for 1999.

The Unix Bug arises from the fact that the standard representation of the time within a Unix system is the number of seconds since 00:00:00 01Jan1970 held in a signed 32 bit long integer. The 32 bit long integer will overflow after 68 years and 18 days (allowing for leap years). For Unix users there will be a crisis sometime in January 2038.

The GPS problem For GPS to work correctly, the GPS satellites and the ground stations need to hold time very accurately indeed. The author understands that there was a GPS clock overflow problem sometime in mid–August 1999. Unless the GPS system is updated in the meantime, the next crisis is expected around May 2019.

One thing is certain: there is a problem. The difficulty is assessing how widespread is the problem. If the problem was just confined to PCs then the PC software suppliers might be persuaded to produce a "bug fix" to cure the problem. The same assertion could be extended to large commercial undertakings who traditionally use large programs written in COBOL or PL/1 running on mainframe computers. The real problems arise in embedded computer systems, such as washing machines, video recorders, vehicle engine management systems, etc.

The "Millennium Bug" becomes an information system security issue because it may well affect the ability of an information system to deliver a service at some time in the future.

12.2 Viruses

The definition of a virus program does not indicate the effects of infestation. There are a number of variants of *virus* programs: one variant uses up a significant proportion of the computer's resources thereby greatly reducing the overall system performance. Other variants of virus programs modify, or even destroy, data files; yet other variants modify or cripple other genuinely useful programs present in the system. The characteristic feature of all virus programs is that they deliberately pass on their destructive powers to all discs in the system.

Luckily, so far, the majority of viruses have been relatively benign: the net effects being a minor degradation of performance of the affected machine coupled with the display of a greeting or other message. However, there are a number of more harmful viruses in circulation which corrupt data, erase files, destroy discs or completely disrupt whole communications networks. However, computer viruses are a potential security threat to any computer installation.

Table 12.1 below attempts to classify the scale and scope of the computer virus problem. It is based on 20 generic viruses recorded between 1970 and the end of 1988. (There were, in fact, many more actual viruses: the majority of the newer viruses are variants of one of the twenty, or so, main families of viruses.) Since the compilation of the table, there have been a few more new generic forms of virus, notably infestations associated with Microsoft Office and Microsoft Exchange which can be spread through e-mail attachments and floppy discs.

Table 12.1: Table showing the distribution of generic viruses.

Effect Environment	Benign	Nuisance	Severe Nuisance	Damaging	Fatal	Totals
IBM PC	1		2	2	1	6
Macintosh	1			1	1	3
Unix Workstns	1			2		3
Mainframes	1	2	2			5
ARPAnet		1			2	3
TOTALS	4	3	4	5	4	20

The *benign* virus does little more than announce its presence; it does not interfere with the functioning of the system. *Nuisance* viruses cause annoyance due to the user repeatedly having to remove unwanted messages from the screen. Viruses classed as *severe nuisances* may modify or destroy data files which will then have to be recreated by repeating the creation process or reloading from CD–ROM. The efficiency of the computer system will

be noticeably decreased by such viruses. *Damaging* viruses actu
data files which will have to be restored from backups. *Fatal* vi
a system completely unusable; after such an attack, the system w
recreation from system installation discs and user data backups. In the worst
cases, the restoration process may take several days to complete and check
out.

It is possible to draw the following conclusions from the data in Table 12.1:

1. All classes of system are vulnerable to computer viruses.
2. IBM PCs (and clones) and similar workstations are particularly susceptible.
3. Viruses on large computer networks can be very damaging and expensive
   to deal with.
4. Mainframes are relatively easy to protect.

Fortunately, in well-managed systems, computer viruses are not the norm.
Much of the fear associated with them is the result of press hype and mis-
informed gossip. However, viruses are still on the increase and it would be
foolish to pretend that they do not exist. More recently, with the advent of
infections carried by e-mail, those sites that consider themselves to be well
protected can no longer afford to be complacent. It would be wise to be aware
of the common symptoms associated with viruses so that an infection can be
recognised when it actually occurs. All the known viruses exhibit one or more
of the following symptoms:

1. unfamiliar graphics or odd messages appear on the screen;
2. programs taking noticeably longer than usual to load;
3. disk accesses seem to be excessive for simple tasks;
4. unusual (but official looking) messages occur more frequently;
5. there is less memory than usual available for user programs;
6. access lights for devices not referenced become lit;
7. programs and/or files mysteriously disappear;
8. executable files change size for no obvious reason;
9. file creation or last update dates change for no obvious reason;
10. disk volume identifiers change for no obvious reason;
11. the number of bad blocks recorded in the FAT increases for no obvious
    reason.

Some of these symptoms require detailed records and some expertise to
recognise correctly. If a normal user suspects that his system has suddenly
become infected, he is strongly advised to get in touch with an expert to
make a detailed diagnosis.

In the descriptions below, I am much indebted to Robert Slade and his
book "A Guide to Computer Viruses"[36]. If you need greater detail and a
more lucid explanation of the virus problem, I would recommend this book;

it appears to be written for the manager who has a technical background rather than for the guru.

12.2.1 Mechanisms

In order that we can determine how best to deal with viruses, it is necessary to have some understanding of the mechanisms that virus programs use to protect themselves and to propagate the infection. A virus is generally composed of three parts:

1. An infection mechanism and a place of residence: this aspect of a virus usually determines how it is recognised and classified.
2. A trigger mechanism: the code to determine when it should be activated to launch the third part.
3. The payload: the code which performs the actions whereby the virus will manifest overt symptoms. This may be something as innocuous as painting a message on the screen to something as destructive as trashing the system disc.

There are four types of virus described here:

1. Boot Sector infector viruses
2. File Infector viruses
3. Companion viruses
4. WORD viruses

12.2.1.1 Boot Sector Infectors (BSIs). BSIs are viruses which base themselves in the boot sector of a disc. In so doing, they can ensure that they are loaded and executed whenever the system is rebooted. Once loaded, these viruses usually stay resident in main memory ready to infect any other discs attached to the system. Once such viruses are loaded, they have to take on the responsibility for completing the loading of the system. To do this, they have to maintain a copy of the original boot block somewhere on the disc. To reduce the risk of detection, they have to do two things: firstly, they should maintain a pretense that the boot sector has not been tampered with; secondly, the presence of the virus should be hidden from the casual observer as far as possible.

The boot sector pretense is maintained by the virus intercepting all attempts to read the boot sector (cylinder 0, surface 0, sector 0) and substituting the address of the copy of the boot sector made when the infection was originally effected. This gives rise to a secondary problem: if the disc were to be reinfected, the effect of the second infection would be to make a copy of an already infected boot sector. Thus any program requesting to read the boot sector would receive an infected copy, thus giving the game away. All "successful" BSIs first check the boot sector of a disc for infection before attempting to infect a disc so as to avoid this particular pitfall.

It is a little more difficult to hide the viral code. There are two possible mechanisms that a virus can use to hide itself:

- The first, and most common, method is for the virus to commandeer the three or so sectors required from the free sector chain and then to transfer these sectors to the bad sector chain. This has the advantage that the operating system will not normally attempt to access such sectors. To counter this, the quality of modern discs is such that damaged sectors, especially on floppy discs, are quite rare. So the presence of bad sectors should be investigated as evidence of possible BSI viruses.
- The second method is for the virus to format an extra cylinder and to write itself into this new space which the operating system knows nothing about. (An 81st cylinder is perfectly feasible on a high density $3\frac{1}{2}$ inch floppy disc.)

The BSI has to intercept all BIOS calls which access discs so as to perform the boot sector substitution trick. This interception gives it the opportunity to monitor all new discs being introduced to the system. These discs are checked for infection. If they are found to be free from infection by the virus code, the virus infects them.

The detection of BSIs is quite complex especially if the viral code is hidden away in an "unofficial" cylinder. The only indication that a BSI may have infected a disc is the unexplained increase of damaged sectors indicated by a disc maintenance program such as scandisk or chkdsk. Some infected discs can be repaired by software (such as Dr Solomon's Magic Bullet). However, it is safer to carry out a complete reformat of the disc so as to ensure that all traces of the virus have been eliminated.

12.2.1.2 File Infectors. "File Infector" viruses differ from BSIs in two ways·

- Firstly, they secrete themselves inside existing program files; and
- secondly, they can be activated only when their host program is loaded and executed.

The general principle of a file infector virus is to arrange for the viral code to be loaded and activated (usually in the form of a *Terminate and Stay Resident* (TSR) program) and then to load the "host" program. How and when the virus performs infections tends to vary with the actual virus, or even with the variant of the virus. Most file infectors look for uninfected ".COM" or ".EXE" files in directories listed in the PATH variable or in standard directories like \DOS and \WIN on discs other than the current one.

The actual infection is achieved by the addition of the viral code to an existing ".COM" or ".EXE" program file. The main problem left is how to make the mechanics of the infection as unobtrusive as possible. The practical options are:

Original File   Infected File

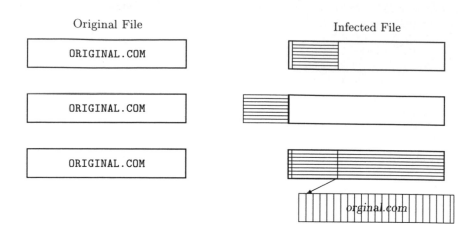

Fig. 12.1: File infection methods

- To overwrite part of the existing program with the viral code. This is
  rather "hit or miss" and may result in the destruction of the host program unless the file infector is very selective in its choice of hosts. The
  advantage of this approach is that the size of the host does not change
  thus making the infection difficult to detect.
- To prepend or append the viral code to the host program. This is the
  most common approach and the simplest to effect successfully. However,
  the size of the program does change – this change in size is easily detected
  by most anti-viral software.
- To copy the actual program into a less visible part of the disc (in a similar
  fashion to a BSI) and replace the original program with the viral code.
  In general, this approach is only feasible with rather small host programs
  up to about 12kB in size. These viruses can be very difficult to detect,
  especially if they use an "unofficial" cylinder in which to store the original
  host program code.

In general, the decontamination of discs from file infectors, once they have
been detected, is quite straightforward. It is merely a matter of replacing the
infected programs with known clean copies. The most important aspect is to
ensure that the clean copies are not inadvertently infected from the infected
disc during the decontamination process.

12.2.1.3 Companion Viruses. "Companion" viruses use the principle
that the COMMAND.COM program searches the PATH directories up to
three times looking for the program corresponding to the command invoked by the user. In the first pass, COMMAND.COM is looking for the
file *xxx*.COM, in the second pass it is looking for the file *xxx*.EXE, and in the

third pass, *xxx*.BAT. The virus effects its infection by changing its own name
to the ".COM" version of a file which exists as a ".EXE" or ".BAT" version
in one of the PATH directories. Thus when the command xxx is invoked, the
virus code will be executed. So as to allay any suspicions of the user, once it
has finished its own work, it attempts to load the genuine program over itself
and execute it.

Companion viruses are quite difficult to detect as they look like any other
".COM" program. The only clue is the co–existence of a "*xxx*.COM" file and
a "*xxx*.EXE" file, possibly in different directories. Currently, there are very
few utilities which even look for any evidence of this form of attack.

This selection does not exhaust the possibilities. There is a virus known
as DIR–II which deposits the viral code in an, as yet, unused part of the
disc. It then copies the directory information of the files it intends to infect
into its own data tables. The infection itself is achieved by overwriting the
start block information in the directory entry with the start block of its own
code. When an infected program is invoked, the viral code is loaded and
executed followed by the virus loading and executing the "infected" file. The
convoluted way in which this virus works makes a straightforward repair of
the infected directory(ies) almost impossible.

12.2.2 WORD Viruses

Microsoft WORD is a word processing package *plus*. It comes with a built in
meta–command processor more powerful than COMMAND.COM as it includes a
full blown macro–processor. WORD creates and updates .DOC files. These files
are generally composed of two parts: a header and a main body. The main
body generally contains the text of which the document is composed. The
header contains commands which configures WORD for the particular document: these commands set up default fonts and document styles and tell
WORD how and where to insert pictures, diagrams and tables held in separate
files created by other programs. The WORD command repertoire includes facilities to create, rename and delete files. There are facilities to create .DOC
files with specially constructed header sections and facilities to edit existing
.DOC file headers.

These facilities have made WORD into a very flexible, useful and popular
word processing package. Unfortunately, these same facilities can be exploited
to create havoc in a DOS/WINDOWS file system. WORD viruses have been
created which consist of .DOC files whose header sections include a set of commands which have all the characteristics of a virus. When the WORD program
loads an "infected" .DOC file, it innocently executes the commands embedded
in the header section. This will include searching for other .DOC files in the
current directory subtree and inserting the virus commands into their header
sections. This is how infection is effected.

WORD keeps a version counter in the header section. This count can be used
as part of a trigger mechanism: for example, if the version exceeds a certain

value or is exactly divisible by a particular prime number, the payload will be launched. The payload typically consists of the deletion of some random files or the trashing of the disc.

In general, WORD viruses range from severe nuisance to fatal, so they should be taken very seriously. Prevention mainly consists of treating *all* foreign WORD .DOC files with extreme care and suspicion. All such files should be submitted to appropriate scanning software before they are allowed anywhere near a production computer system.

WORD viruses are such a recent phenomenon that there are no completely reliable disinfectant programs. Current disinfectant programs can deal with the more common infestations. However, mutations of WORD viruses appear so quickly and frequently, there is no guarantee of complete disinfestation. Consequently, if a .DOC file is found to be infected the file should be deleted and reloaded from a backup. In a dire emergency, the body of the .DOC file might be rescued by attempting to use another non–Microsoft word processor package to import the file and then save it in a non–WORD format file.

The moral of this is:

- Use scanning software regularly and frequently to check all WORD files.
- Make frequent backups of all (scanned) WORD files.
- Treat all foreign WORD files with extreme care.

12.3 Virus Examples

12.3.1 The "Brain" virus

The "Brain" virus is probably the oldest MS–DOS virus. It is a boot sector infector virus; it is very virulent and very widespread. There are many variants of the "Brain" virus: in particular, the "Den Zuk" and the "Monkey" viruses are both quite close relations.

The viral code occupies three disc sectors. One sector replaces the boot sector (which is copied to another part of the disc), together with two others which contain the main code of the virus. All three blocks are disguised by being made part of the "bad block chain" which is almost completely ignored by MS–DOS and user programs.

The original "Brain" virus was relatively innocuous: it merely changed the volume label and would only infect 360kB floppy discs. It completely ignored hard discs. These reassuring remarks do not apply to some of the later variants. In particular, most variants are not so choosy as to what sort of disc they try to infect. Many fail to calculate correctly the disc geometry and write themselves over part of the FAT.

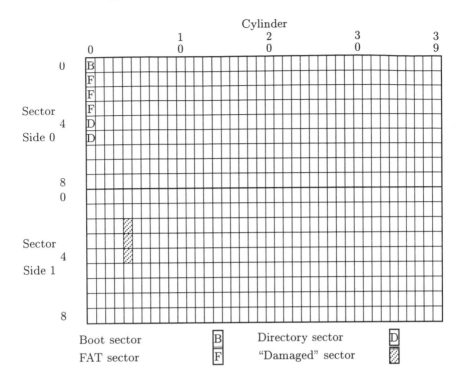

Fig. 12.2: The "Brain" Virus

12.3.2 The "Lehigh" Virus

The "Lehigh" virus dates back to 1987. Its importance is not that it was particularly terrible or widespread but that it was the virus that stimulated the research effort into dealing with the virus threat.

This virus only infected COMMAND.COM files. This it achieved by writing its code into the stack space at the top end of the COMMAND.COM file. Infection of other discs was effected when an uninfected disc was accessed by a normal DOS command (e.g. TYPE, COPY or DIR). It would not attempt to reinfect an already infected COMMAND.COM file. After four successful infections, the virus would scribble over the Indexboot sector and FAT of its own disc, thereby making it unusable (and at the same time committing suicide!). This behaviour pattern ensured that it was not a very virulent virus and that it did not spread very far.

12.3.3 The "Jerusalem" Virus

The "Jerusalem" virus is the most widespread and has the most variants of any of the known computer viruses. The "Jerusalem" family of virus programs infect both .EXE and .COM programs. It copes very successfully with .COM files by prepending itself to the .COM file. It is not quite so successful with .EXE files as it is apt to continuously reinfect .EXE files so that they get larger and larger. Each infection increases the size of the file by 1813 bytes. ("1813" is another common name for this virus). Worse still, more complex .EXE files with overlays tend to confuse it and cause it to insert its code into the wrong place in the file.

The payload of the "Jerusalem" virus tends to vary. One strain had a payload that waited until the occurrence of Friday 13th and would then delete files. Not unsurprisingly, this strain became known as "Friday the 13th".

12.3.4 The "CHRISTMA EXEC"

"EXEC" files are the IBM mainframe equivalent of MS–DOS ".BAT" files. The "CHRISTMA EXEC" consists of an "EXEC" file embedded in an e–mail message. It was invoked by the unsuspecting recipient browsing through the message and typing `Christmas` or `Christma`. This would result in an ASCII Xmas tree being output to the screen and, at the same time, the user's "NAMES" and "NETLOG" files for the e–mail addresses on any accounts that the user had received mail from or had sent mail to. Thus the electronic equivalent of a chain letter was set up which would effectively choke the communications network and eventually fill up the various user discs with useless e–mail files. The main impact of this worm was felt mainly in IBM's own internal network between 9th and 12th December 1987.

12.3.5 The "Love Letter" Worm

The "Love Letter" worm (it is technically a *worm* since the preferred infestation method was through the Internet) appeared early in May 2000. Within a week it had spread to nearly 1000 sites and may have affected nearly half a million individual computer systems. The virus code was written in Visual Basic and was carried in the header of an attached Microsoft Office document named `LOVE-LETTER-FOR-YOU.TXT.VBS`. The way it was distributed almost guaranteed that the recipient would open the attachment thereby causing the local machine to become infected.

The act of opening the attachment triggered further infestation as follows:

- It would search the local disc for ".VBE" or ".VBS" files (and possibly others). The contents of the targeted files would be replaced by a copy of the virus code.
- It would search for IRC (Internet Relay Chat) files. The system would be amended so that if an innocent person joined a chat room in use by the victim, a copy of the virus code would be forwarded silently to the new chat participant.

- It would then use the Microsoft Outlook address lists to e-mail copies of itself to every e-mail address in the address list.

This latter step was a stroke of misguided genius on the part of the worm implementor since the innocent recipient would most probably know the supposed sender and would assume that the e-mail was quite innocent. The "Love Letter" infestation was so virulent that many sites had to close down their mail servers while the whole of the local area network was being disinfected.

12.4 Dealing with Viruses

Obviously, **prevention** is better than **cure**. The defence against computer viruses needs to be considered under two headings: precautions against infection in the first place, and how to get rid of an infection once it has occurred. Protection against infection cannot be guaranteed if the system in question reads discs written to by other (suspect) machines, or if the system is connected by communication lines to other (suspect) machines.

12.4.1 Anti–Viral Software

Suitably written software can be used to warn the user of a suspicious event, which could be part of an attempt to infect a disc or a file, to prevent certain types of infection, to scan a system for signs of infection and to disinfect a file or disc from infection. There are many forms of anti–viral software on the market. The problem is to make the most appropriate selection for any particular circumstance. Only one thing is certain in this field: despite all the claims of the ad men, there is no single package which can provide total protection, diagnosis and cure for all virus problems.

Anti–viral software can be grouped into four functional areas:

Activity monitors: this is software installed to monitor interactions between software and the system so that it can warn against, or even prevent, any suspicious activity. A common example of this is a BIOS monitor which prevents any program from writing to the boot sector of any disc. In this case, the monitor has to be disabled when a new version of the operating system is being installed. Despite their sophistication, they are not always effective in preventing an infection. For example, boot sector monitors are very effective against the early BSIs; however, some more recent BSIs have learnt to avoid the use of BIOS calls to effect disc writes and so they are not detected by such boot sector monitors.

Change detection software: the principle behind change detection software is that it maintains a database of all system resources, discs (including their system areas) and files, etc.; in that database there is a

corresponding list of CRC checksums. Periodically, usually when the system is rebooted – otherwise daily, the checksums of these resources are recomputed and compared with the stored values. An alarm is raised if any change is detected. The main problem with such software is that it is rather too effective; there are too many false alarms raised due to users failing to notify the software database of legitimate changes to the system. A second problem with such software is that when it does detect a suspicious change, it cannot determine the cause or the software responsible for the change.

Scanning software: this is software that is run (usually manually) to detect the presence, or otherwise, of an infection. It examines memory, boot sectors and files looking for viral signatures, sequences of instructions that are known to be in certain virus programs but not in most other programs. Because signature databases need to be updated on a monthly, or even a weekly, basis, this technique is only suitable for use against known viruses. It also suffers from not being able to prevent an infection; it is only effective once a system has been already infected. Despite these drawbacks, scanning software is perhaps the most useful of the viral detection techniques; scanning should be carried out daily so that any successful infections are detected and dealt with before they have a chance to get a hold on the system and do severe damage.

Disinfectant software: as the name implies, this is the software used to remove an infection from a disc or program that has been infected. Depending on the complexity of the virus, this software will have differing degrees of success.

12.4.2 Anti–Viral Precautions

The following precautions will materially reduce the risk of infection:

1. Make frequent and regular backups of all vital program and data files. The uninfected backups will form the basis of any recovery procedure.
2. Write protect any disc which does not have to be written to.
3. Set up a *quarantine* machine which has no hard disc for the sole purpose of checking and decontaminating imported discs using appropriate virus scanning and decontamination software.
4. Treat all imported discs with the maximum of suspicion – all discs new to the system should be copied to clean discs, file by file, via RAM (using the mechanism invoked when a system only has one floppy disc) – this reduces the risk of importing Viruses distributed via boot blocks and "bad" blocks.
5. Where possible, discs created by the mechanism described above, should be scrutinised for viruses by an expert or a trusted propriety virus detection program.

6. Absolutely forbid the casual import of software, particularly computer games from unknown third parties, particularly public bulletin boards.
7. All users should be fully briefed of the risks from viruses and should be informed of the need for security procedures and of what they consist.

12.4.3 Virus Decontamination

Once a computer virus infection has been recognised, there is a need to eradicate the infection as quickly and as cheaply as possible. The following procedures are relatively simple but actually require a trained person to carry them out quickly and effectively:

1. Firstly, isolate the infected machine and all its associated discs from all other machines in the locality.
2. Boot from a clean (expendable) floppy DOS system disc before carrying out the actions listed below.
3. If the infected machine has a hard disc, carry out a complete "software" reformat of the hard disc (i.e., what would be known elsewhere as a "file system re-initialisation") – this will mean the destruction of ALL the programs and data held on the disc. (Hopefully, the hard disc was backed up fairly recently!) Do not be tempted to use any of the "fast" reformatting options; you must ensure that every block on the disc is overwritten, that the disc is scanned for bad blocks so that the bad block list is recalculated from scratch and, in particular, that the boot block is reset with safe contents.
4. Carry out a full "software" reformat on all floppy discs suspected of being contaminated.
5. Create a new set of discs by making copies of backup discs known to be absolutely free of infection.
6. Attempt to determine how the virus was introduced into the system. If necessary, tighten up local procedures so as to reduce the risk of re-infection.
7. Check whether any potentially infected discs or tapes have been exported to other systems. If there are any such other infected systems, carry out this procedure (recursively) on every system which may have been contaminated by disc exports.

12.5 Java & Active–X

Sun Microsystems introduced Java in about 1995. The original intention of Java was to provide additional functionality to be given to documents on the World Wide Web (WWW). The main intention was to provide mechanisms to allow simple menus, form filling and animation. It was also capable of providing sound effects (audio). The Microsoft Corporation responded with an equivalent proprietary mechanism, Active–X. From the security viewpoint, the two systems are almost equivalent in terms of the threats posed. The main difference between them is that Java was put by Sun into the public domain whereas Active–X is a proprietary product.

Java is essentially a full programming language supported by a large, well documented application library. Java differs from most programming languages in that instead of the Java translator generating the computer's native machine code, it generates a standard *intercode* which is then interpreted by a special program known as an *interpreter*. The source code of the interpreter is publicly available, which means that the Java interpreter can be implemented on almost any type of computer. This, in turn, means that I can write a Java program on my computer and send it to anyone I choose, confident that the program can be run on the recipient's computer. The Netscape Navigator program has a Java interpreter built into it. Small Java fuctions which can be passed between computers are sometimes known as *applets*.

The threat arises from the fact that there are no practical limits to the functionality of a Java program. The standard Java library provides comprehensive support for system programming so that Java programs can control hardware devices, such as audio devices to produce sound. This facility allows Java programs to control other devices such as discs and communication ports thus effectively bypassing some protection mechanisms in the far machine. This can be fatal in computers controlled by MSDOS, Windows or Windows95. In Unix systems, a user and his files are not protected from a rogue Java program but the operating system and its protected resources should be safe, but only provided it is *not* the *superuser* (root) executing the Java program.

This threat is so severe that there is a restricted version of Java which disables some of the more dangerous library features. With Java protection enabled, this is essentially the version of Java to be found in Netscape. This restriction is sufficient to make most simple applets safe. However, it is no protection against a malicious applet which has embedded within it some of the dangerous Java library support routines. Hence, in Netscape, there is an option to disallow the execution of applets received from another computer.

In principle, what is said about Java applies also to Active–X. From this discussion we can deduce some simple principles to reduce the risks posed by Java or Active–X programs received from another computer:

- Never attempt to execute an imported program if you are logged in as a privileged user (*root, superuser* or *administrator*).
- As a normal user, only attempt to execute an imported program if you are confident that it is safe to do so.
- If you are executing an Internet browser such as Netscape or Internet Explorer, disable the facility to execute imported applets.

The effect of these guidlines is to disable the use of multi–media over the Internet.

12.6 The "Millennium Bug"

The first priority here is to recognise that there is a "millennium bug" problem and to determine the extent of the problem. This section is mainly composed of a check list which should cover most of the issues. This discussion is restricted to the effects of the "millennium bug" on information systems and is not concerned with embedded computer technology to found in cars, domestic goods or even medical equipment.

Before 1st January 2000, the simplest way to check for the problem was to make a copy of the system and carry out a live test. It was a mistake to perform such tests on an operational system since, if it was not millennium compliant, the system may have beeen made irreversibly unusable. If there were no anomalous side effects, then there was some confidence that there was no great problem.

As it happened, most of the disasters that many people predicted did not happen; to many people, the "millennium bug" turned out to be a non–event. Much of the credit for the non–event must go to the effort put into the preparation for the event over the previous two years or so. However, despite all the preparation and testing, there were some anomolies which only came to light after the turn of the year 2000. One of the more amusing ones was a UK local education authority which sent invitations to local centenarians to enrole for kindergarten school in the autumn of 2000.

The GPS roll-over event in August 1999 passed with hardly a mention in the papers. The predictions of ships heading merrily into cliffs and aircraft getting lost turned out to be too pessimistic; these events just did not happen Again the credit for this must go to the preparations made to avoid any possible disastrous consequences of the roll-over event.

The "millennium bug" crisis is still far from over: many of the fixes are temporary. In many cases, application programs have been fixed so that year dates in the range 00 to 49 lie in the 21st century while dates in the range 50 to 99 remain in the 20th century. The "millennium bug" is going to rear its head again in the future when most people have forgotten all about it. There is going to be another GPS roll-over early in the year 2019 and there is still the Unix roll-over event to come in 2038. By that time, all operating systems should be at least 64 bit compliant. However, the same assertion cannot be made for many of the applications still running in 2038. When that time comes, the "millennium bug" of 2000 will be a distant memory. One hopes that the world will not be caught unawares.

Assuming that some tests were, in fact, carried out there may be some anomolies. In such a case it would be necessary to do more work to identify where the problems really lay. The most likely areas to look into are:

The computer itself. Computers, especially PCs, have built-in software or firmware (e.g., the PC BIOS) which provide clock/calendar services. Some older machines may not have "millennium compliant" versions. For PCs, there are programs available which will test the hardware/firmware for millennium compliance. For other machines, e.g., Sun workstations or Silicon Graphics workstations, consult the manufacturer's support departments. For recently manufactured machines (1997 onwards) there should be no problem as most system designers have been aware of the problem for several years. There should be a simple upgrade, a change of BIOS or EEPROM, for recent machines which fail the millennium compliance test. There may be no such simple solution for older machines (more than four or so years old); such machines may have to be replaced altogether.

Soft centred peripherals. Some peripheral devices have built-in calendar services:

- some alphanumeric VDUs have built-in calendar chips
- RAID disc controllers
- complex peripheral devices such as ATMs

Unless these peripherals get the date/time from the host computer, they will need to be assessed separately.

Bought in COTS Software. Enquiries with the supplier may produce help and a guide as to which versions have been tested for millennium compliance. Failing that, if the host computer can be shown to be millennium compliant, then changing the date and carrying out extensive tests may one some confidence in the software.

Bought in bespoke software. If it is possible to communicate with the designers and programmers it should be possible to get the required information. It may mean that a contract will have to be raised for remedial work to make the software millennium compliant. The real problem arises when testing indicates that software is not millennium compliant and the software designers and programmers are no longer accessible. In the worst case, the software will have to be scrapped and new compliant software commissioned.

Locally written software. It is assumed in this case that it is possible to access the design and implementation documentation and the source code of the software. Under these conditions, it should be possible to determine exactly how millennium compliant the software is, and how to effect any necessary enhancements.

Determining the scale of the problem is the first step. In theory, once the actual problem has been determined, it should be comparatively simple to implement a solution. Unfortunately, there is a world shortage of the skilled programmers needed to implement the necessary remedies. Consequently, wise managers are already planning work arounds for the next manifestations of the "millennium bug".

12.7 Summary

Computer viruses and other related software threats are a problem. The risks associated with these threats can be materially reduced by the implementation of fairly simple and inexpensive precautions. Once a case of infection has been recognised, a fairly simple set of draconian drills must be employed to ensure the eradication of the infection. The cost of such drills can be kept to a reasonable minimum by the simple expedient of frequent and regular disc backups.

The "millennium bug" could have been a serious problem. Variants of it could pose a serious problem at some time in the future. The careful preparations made to avoid the worst effects of such a bug demonstrate that effort expended in advance of a known (potential) problem is well worthwhile. By analogy, in the case of viruses (which are a more frequent event than "millennium bugs"), planning and prevention are almost certainly cheaper than waiting for the problem to materialise and then having to effect a cure.

Chapter 13

The UK Data Protection Acts

The advent of computer systems enabled governments and commercial undertakings to collect, amass and process information concerning individuals, their private lives and their employment. Unfortunately, this activity was not regulated and there were a number of notorious abuses of this information both by governmental and commercial organisations. These abuses generally took the form of the organisation taking arbitrary action based on errors in the information held about the victims. The most common of these abuses seemed to emanate from credit agencies and social security offices.

As a response to continued public outcry against the worst of these abuses, most western democracies were forced to enact legislation to protect individuals from abuses by organisations holding data on them. The British *Data Protection Act* was the United Kingdom's legislation to protect the British citizen from such abuse.

The British Data Protection Acts embody eight basic principles. These principles, enumerated below, are generally similar to those embodied in equivalent legislation in most other western countries. This chapter is not concerned with the niceties of the law, but in the security implications of these general principles.

In essence, the UK Data Protection Act (1984) stated that a person or an organisation may only hold personal data (i.e., data which pertains to an identifiable individual) if the person or organisation has registered that the personal data is being held and the specific purpose or purposes for which the data is being held. The 1984 Act created a post of *Data Protection Registrar* (now called the *Information Commissioner*) who is responsible for administering the scheme and approving every request by applicants to hold personal data. The act lays down conditions which limit what can be done with personal data.

The Data Protection Act (1998) came into force in March 2001 and su-
perceded the 1984 act. In general, for someone who is not a lawyer and is not
directly responsible for the administration of its provisions, the importance of
the 1998 Data protection Act can be summed up in a couple of sentences: it
reinforced the 1984 Data Protection Act and closed off some of its loop holes.
The most important of its innovations was to extend its scope to all forms of
data whether held in human readable form (e.g. on paper) or electronically.

This chapter briefly outlines the main provisions of the UK Data Protection Acts and then discusses the information security implications of the
Acts. Some of the the detail of the UK Data Protection Acts may not be
relevant in other jurisdictions; however, the associated information security
principles are almost certainly relevent in any jurisdiction.

13.1 Definitions

The Data Protection Acts very carefully limit their scope by defining a number of terms:

The data subject is an individual who is the subject of *personal data*.

The data user is the person or organisation who "holds" the data.

Personal data meaning data consisting of information which relates to a
   living individual (the data subject) who can be identified from that information, including any opinions held about that individual.

Sensitive personal data is data which relates to an identifiable individual
   consisting of any of the following:
   - the racial or ethnic origin of the data subject;
   - the political opinions of the data subject;
   - the religious beliefs of the data subject;
   - the physical or mental health of the data subject;
   - the sexual life of the data subject;
   - whether the data subject is a member of a trade union or similar
     organisation;
   - any offence, alleged offence, associated legal proceedings or court
     sentence pertaining to the data subject.

The specified purpose is the purpose, declared to the Data Protection
   Commissioner, for which the personal data is collected and held.

Processing in this context means, in respect of personal data, any of the
   following:
   - the obtaining, recording and holding of data;
   - the organisation, sorting, adaption or alteration of the data;
   - the retrieval, consultation or any other use of the data;
   - the merging, splitting, deletion or destruction of the data.

The most important of these definitions is that of the **data subject**. The act only applies to information which can be associated with a living human. It does not apply to anonymously held information. For example, if data collected for an opinion poll is held without any mechanism for the pollsters being able to identify the individuals who participated then the act does not apply. If participants can be identified, even if it is through some code or index number, then the act does apply. The second important definition is the scope of the term *sensitive personal data*. If the information held by the user includes any sensitive personal data then there are security implications as to the care which needs to be applied with respect to the holding of such data.

13.2 The Data Protection Principles

The eight principles of the Data Protection Act are:

The first principle: states that "the information to be contained in personal data shall be obtained, and personal data shall be processed, fairly and lawfully",

The second principle: states that "personal data shall be held only for one or more specified and lawful purpose or purposes".

The third principle states that "personal data held for any purpose or purposes shall not be used or disclosed in any manner incompatible with that purpose or those purposes".

The fourth principle: states that "personal data held for any purpose or purposes shall be adequate, relevant and not excessive in relation to that purpose or those purposes".

The fifth principle: states that "personal data shall be accurate and, where necessary, kept up to date".

The sixth principle: states that "personal data held for any purpose or purposes shall not be kept for longer than is necessary for that purpose or those purposes".

The seventh principle: states that "an individual shall be entitled:
  (a) at reasonable intervals and without undue delay or expense –
    (i) to be informed by any data user whether he holds personal data of which that individual is the subject; and
    (ii) to access to any such data held by a data user;
    and
  (b) where appropriate, to have such data corrected or erased".

The eighth principle: states that "appropriate security measures shall be taken against unauthorised access to, or alteration, disclosure or destruction of, personal data, and against accidental loss or destruction of personal data".

13.2.1 The First Principle

This principle is concerned with the "fairness" and the legality of the collection and use of personal data. The first principle states that personal data may be only collected for an approved purpose under the Act. Further, "sensitive" personal information may only be collected under very restricted conditions and only then, under normal circumstances, with the explicit approval of the "subject".

The "fairness" implies that the information cannot be obtained by trickery; when the information is being collected, the "subject" should be informed of the reasons for the collection of the data. It should outlaw such practices as taking a customer's personal details for the supposed purpose of registering newly-purchased equipment for guarantee purposes and then using the information for sales mailshots. The legal restriction implies that information may not be obtained by such means as phone tapping or the interception of mail.

13.2.2 The Second Principle

This principle restricts the use of personal data to those uses specified and declared in the submission to the Data Protection Registrar and approved by the Registrar. This means that if the "user" has legally obtained personal information for a specific purpose then it may not be used for any other (undeclared) purpose. This principle is essentially a management issue and has no security implications.

13.2.3 The Third Principle

This principle reinforces the second principle and, further, forbids the disclosure of any personal data to an unauthorised person or body. This principle implies that for the specified use there must be a restricted number of persons who have access to the personal information. This, in turn, implies that the "user" must implement security mechanisms so as to restrict the personal information to those who have a need to have access to it.

This restriction needs to be implemented at two levels: firstly, procedurally, authorised persons should not communicate any personal information to unauthorised colleagues or outsiders; secondly, any computer system should be configured so that users should not be able to access personal data to which they are not entitled.

13.2.4 The Fourth Principle

This principle declares that the data collected should be appropriate and sufficient for the specified use(s) and that data not needed should not be collected or kept. This principle is essentially a management issue. The only security implication is the matter of culling data that is no longer needed (see also the sixth principle below).

13.2.5 The Fifth Principle

This principle declares that any data held should be accurate and up to date. This principle is a management issue and has no security implications.

13.2.6 The Sixth Principle

This principle declares that any personal data should not be kept for any longer than is necessary for the specified use(s). This principle has security implications in that it implies that the "user" must implement data culling mechanisms and procedures.

13.2.7 The Seventh Principle

This principle declares that a "subject" is entitled to know if a "user" holds any data concerning the "subject"; to know what it is, and, if it is wrong, to have it corrected or even erased altogether. This principle is a management issue and has no security implications.

13.2.8 The Eighth Principle

This principle instructs the "user" to care for any personal data, to safeguard it against accidental or unauthorised changes or deletion, and to prevent unauthorised persons or bodies obtaining access to it. This principle is there to ensure that all the security issues are covered. It reinforces the security implications of the third, fourth and sixth principles. It also forces the user to implement appropriate backup and anti–hacking mechanisms and procedures.

13.3 Summary

Data protection legislation has important implications for the information security of an organisation. In particular, the organisation is legally bound to implement security measures which ensure that the integrity of any personal data is maintained and that access to personal data, particularly sensitive personal data, is confined to those employees who actually have a need to access it. It also imposes on the user organisation the obligation to implement a culling mechanism and associated procedures, and to carry them out, so as to ensure that data is only kept for as long as it is required for its registered purpose.

Chapter 14

System Administration and Security

No information security can rely on the standard list of physical, personnel and technical security measures. Unfortunately, unless the information system is diligently administered, the quality of the system security will rapidly deteriorate. This is an inconvenient aspect of security all too often overlooked by politicians and administrators trying to cut costs.

The list of administrative tasks which are applicable to an information system is endless. However, the most important which need to be carried out properly are:

- system procurement;
- system and data backups;
- resource management and tracking;
- system testing and probing;
- configuration management;
- system change control;
- database administration;
- user account management; and
- audit trail management.

These topics will be considered in turn below.

14.1 The Procurement of Secure Information Systems

Any information system needs to be procured. In an ideal situation, the information system is procured from scratch. In practice, there is a heritage system to deal with. The practices and the (data) resources of the old system will have a strong influence on the new system. On top of that, the old system needs to be kept going during the procurement process. In the interests of simplicity, these complications are ignored in the discussion below. This does not mean that the procedure outlined below is entirely useless; it does mean that, almost certainly, the practitioner will need to amend the procedure to suit the circumstances that prevail.

The greatest temptation, when asked to procure and implement an information system with security implications, is to get totally immersed in high tech security techniques before there has been any analysis as to exactly what the problem is. This can only result in disaster: an expensive and complex solution to a problem that may not even exist.

All too often the problem is made worse because the "security experts" brought in to advise have little to gain from proposing common sense, low tech solutions. In some cases, much of their income derives from commission arising from subsequent equipment, software and consultancy contracts.

To counter these possibilities, it is necessary to follow a simple methodology which will ensure that issues are addressed in a logical order, and that the costs are kept down to a reasonable minimum. It is the purpose of this chapter to propose and elaborate on one such methodology.

14.1.1 The Requirement

The first step in any project, whether it involves IT or not, is to establish the requirement. In this context, this means interpreting a goal, expressed in terms of senior management generalities, in a system specification:

- scope the *problem*;
- establish the *purpose* of the system;
- who provides the *inputs* (data) for the system and how the data enters the system?
- Who *benefits* from the system?
- What is the *value* of the data in the system?

This can be achieved by the use of a *soft systems* methodology, such as Wilson's SSM stages I and II [47]. A discussion on requirement elicitation methodologies is beyond the scope of this book. What can be said is that effort invested in requirements analysis early in a project is repaid by saved money and effort in the later implementation stages of the project.

14.1.2 The Outline Security Policy

From the requirements analysis it should be possible to determine the basic security requirements for the proposed information system:

- Who will own the system and, hence, will be responsible for funding the security measures?

- What features of the system need protection?
- What are the perceived threats to the system?
- What resources are available to protect the system?

From the answers to these questions, it should be possible to draft a preliminary (draft) security policy document along the lines of Appendix D in a precise form.

14.1.3 Hardware Selection

The selection and purchase of computer hardware is much easier than it used to be ten or so years ago. The main reason for this is that the number of available computer architecture families has been reduced from 30 or so fifteen years ago down to about 6 at the turn of the millennium. Of the six, only one, the Intel x86 architecture, is widely available from several manufacturers. The remainder are confined to single manufacturers or small consortia of manufacturers. Most of the six are capable of being configured to provide roughly equivalent high levels of performance.

Casting aside prejudice and other emotive arguments, the choice of architecture should be governed by:

- the cost of porting any heritage software to the chosen architecture;
- the availability of long term support for the chosen architecture;
- the availability of human expertise to configure and manage the hardware of the chosen architecture;
- the life costs of the hardware of the chosen architecture.

Computers based on Intel x86 processors are the most widely available and are generally fairly cheap to acquire. However, when support and whole life costs are taken into account, other architectures, e.g., IBM Power PC or Sun SPARC, may be more desirable.

14.1.4 Software Selection

There used to be a belief that publically available software would be unsuitable for use in a secure environment. As a result, governments and large corporations insisted that software used in their more sensitive applications had to be written either in-house or by a software house under contract. Such software is known as *bespoke* software. The fallacy in that belief is that the user base for such software is very restricted. It follows then that the amount of testing and use such software receives will be less than similar software on sale to the general public.

Over the last fifteen years or so, there has been a growing belief that COTS software will be inherently more reliable than any bespoke software. The justification for such a belief is that a large user base will rapidly discover any errors or weaknesses in COTS software and will use commercial pressures to get the errors removed.

At the start of the 21st century, there is a growing belief that the best software is *open source* software. The source code of open source software, as its name implies, is available for the public to view and, where appropriate, amend. When errors manifest themselves, work-arounds and repairs are usually available within a matter of days. This is in contrast to closed source software, where the typical turn-round time for software re–issues is three months. Because of the very rapid turn-round time, the reliability of open source software rises five to ten times faster than commercial closed source software.

It is difficult to generalise as to the relative merits of commercial software and open source software. It would not be true to say that all open source software is more reliable than its commercial equivalents for two reasons: firstly, the very best commercial software is the equal of the very best open source software; secondly, open source software has not been around long enough and is not sufficiently available for a valid comparison to be made.

From this discussion we can deduce that bespoke software should be used only as a last resort: such software is expensive and generally less trustworthy than the alternatives. The choice between the use of commercial software and open source software should be governed by such factors as the level of support required for the software and the viability of the organisation supporting the software. The final choice should be determined by the suitability of the software for the required application and the requirements and skills of the software users.

14.1.5 Certified Software

It may be thought that the use of certified software would solve many procurement problems. Apart from the additional acquisition costs involved, there are, potentially, a number of drawbacks to the use of such software:

- It costs a lot of money and effort to test and certify software. Consequently, not every version of a software system will be subjected to the certification process. This, in turn, means that there will be very infrequent upgrades to the software which may mean being restricted to rather out of date hardware systems and software applications until there is a new certified release of the software.
- The certification process will almost certainly restrict some of the system functionality, in some cases to the extent that some applications cannot run as intended.
- Certified systems have a tendency to be less user-friendly than their uncertified counterparts. At the very least, the user will be forced to authenticate himself to the system via a password before certain operations are

permitted. Typically, there will be restrictions on such natural facilities as "cut and paste".

Such are the inconveniences of certified software users, not fully committed to the needs of the security policy, will find ways of circumventing these restrictions.

There is another issue in connection with certified software. Compared to the full choice of software available, there are very few certified packages. The credibility of the certification authorities is, to a certain extent, determined by the number of certified packages. If every package submitted for certification gets a certificate, then there would seem to be little point in the certification process. If the certification criteria are so strict that no packages gain a certificate, the certification process has no practical value. The certifiers are then presented with a dilemma: how strict should they be with the assessment? Usually, the general public are only aware that a package has a certificate or not; generally, they cannot get access to the report written by the assessors which supported the certification process. In the case of government official certification, the general public may not even be aware of the actual level of certification. (Normally, government project managers are made aware of certification levels and can be briefed on the contents of relevant assessment reports.)

The use of certified software cannot be used as a blanket solution to software quality control problems. Such software should only be used if it is known to solve a specific security problem.

14.1.6 Summary

The procurement of an IT system is far from straightforward. The greatest danger is to attempt to solve the apparently simple problems first, for example, go out and buy a computer system before the exact purpose of the computer system has been established. This approach has been shown to be the start of the slippery slope to an expensive disaster by countless examples in the government area and similar fiascos in some commercial organisations.

Nearly all non–trivial successful IT systems have been built from a baseline where the requirement has been studied and well understood. Equally importantly, the technical aspects of the security policy need to be determined before any design can be completed. Only then is the implementation team in a position to choose the appropriate technology to solve the actual problem.

14.2 System and Data Backups

The primary aim of a backup strategy should be to facilitate the rapid restoration of service after a disaster. Other possible benefits from a backup strategy can be the recovery of an old and trusted version of a file after some unsuccessful experimentation. There are a number of basic strategies:

- regular 100% backups;
- regular backups of those files which have changed since the previous 100% backup – this form of backup is usually called an *incremental backup*;
- backups consisting of sets of editing commands which will convert a reference set of files to the current set of files; such backups are sometimes called *delta backups*;
- disc mirroring (RAID 1).

The simplest of these to implement and manage is the regular 100% backups. However, if the system is of any size, the backup will take a long time (typically 20 minutes per GByte) and will consume large numbers of tapes (which will have to be stored somewhere!). Such backups should only be carried out infrequently, every quarter, say, or monthly at most. There is one part of an information system which does not change at all frequently: the system software. It is usual to backup all the system software only when it is installed or updated. All other backups only involve the system data.

When 100% backups are effected, it is normal for a full duplicate backup to be made: one is kept as a local primary backup and the other is taken to a physically remote site in case the local system is destroyed by a fire or other major disaster.

Incremental backups are a compromise between convenience and performance. The greatest disadvantage of incremental backups is the complexity of keeping track of which tape holds the backup copy of any particular file.

Delta backups are very complex and require specialist software systems for them to work reliably. One such system is the Unix "Workbench" otherwise known as the *Source Code Control System* (SCCS). It is not suitable for use as the main backup subsystem of a computer system; however, it does provide a reliable mechanism to allow a user to recover any version of a file that is subject to regular change.

When backup tapes are created, files from many parts of the system are copied onto these tapes. The tapes then take on the classification of the most sensitive files held by the system. Consequently all backup tapes should be protected appropriately.

A backup strategy should form part of any system security policy in support of the maintenance of a specified level of service. There is no universal ideal backup strategy; each system requires a strategy designed to maintain the required level of service from the information system.

14.3 Resource Tracking and Management

The most common security procedure is a mechanism to keep track of people and documents associated with sensitive systems. It is sensible to confine sensitive material to a particular area. It would also be sensible to choose an area so that access to it can be easily controlled; in particular, the physical access arrangements should be such that only those people who have right of access to the sensitive area should be able to get in. Once access control has been established, there should be a recording mechanism which indicates who is actually in the sensitive area at any one time. Inspection of this record at the end of the working day should indicate which visitors are still in the restricted area. The ultimate long term purpose of such a record is to provide basic information to an enquiry team investigating a breach of security.

There should be a mechanism which allows management to keep track of sensitive documents. This is normally achieved by means of a document register; the register is a book in which there is an entry for every sensitive document. Each entry should record:

- the title of the document;
- an indication of how sensitive the document is and any restrictions as to who may have access to it;
- the date of creation of the document and who was the originator;
- the current location of the document.

Each document entry should be maintained until the document is destroyed. If such a document register is to be maintained seriously, the register itself requires regular checking. Normal good practice is for a check of 5% of the register entries on a monthly basis. If a document cannot be found in the location indicated in the register then a search for it should be started. If the document still cannot be located within an hour then it should be deemed to be outside the control of the custodian, in other words, lost.

The term *document* covers anything from a single page memorandum to a complete book. The term also covers computer magnetic media such as magnetic tapes, floppy discs and hard discs.

14.4 System Testing and Probing

It is not sufficient to install a "secure" system and then sit back and watch it "do its work". Unfortunately, threats to the system do not stand still. For a system manager to be confident that his system is secure, he must have tested it against some of the most sophisticated attack software that is available. There are packages such as `satan` and `crack` which subject a (Unix, NT or VMS) system to a variety of tests:

- Is the file system configured securely? (i.e., are file and directory permits sensible?)
- Are only the authorised system programs endowed with system privileges? Are they identical to the original distributed programs?
- Have the patches which close off known security holes been installed?
- Are there any system privileged scripts (batch files)?
- Are users undermining system security with .rhost files?
- Are users using sensible passwords? Are they changing them regularly?

By running such packages on a regular basis, the system management will get regular reports on the effectiveness of their security administration.

14.5 Configuration Management

Any practical information system will change and develop in the course of its life. In a system with security implications, it is important to keep track of the system inventory and to control changes to the system. Such is the pace of development of IT, it is seldom practical to keep the configuration unchanged through the life of the system. The two most important reasons for this are:

- Once the system enters service, the user requirement is almost certain to change and there are bound to be errors in the system requiring correction.
- Software suppliers normally produce upgrades every year or so. A by-product of this is that support for the old version of the software is usually withdrawn within three months of the issue of the new software.

The standard approach to managing the system configuration is to form a System Configuration Control Committee (SCCC). The terms of reference of the SCCC are:

- to catalogue the hardware and software assets of the system;
- to assess all requests for changes and upgrades for their effects on security, functionality and costs;
- to assess the implementation proposals for any approved change requests for practicality and security implications;
- to assess the correctness and conformance of any actual change to the approved design before giving the change final approval for incorporation into the system;
- to ensure that the system asset register is updated to reflect the new configuration.

Configuration management is an essential tool in maintaining the effectiveness of the security mechanisms of an information system throughout its life. Beginning the configuration management while the system is being developed, before it goes live, will greatly reduce the difficulties of implementing such a system. It is highly desirable, if it can be arranged, for the members of the eventual SCCC to be seconded to the implementor's (contractor's) Project Change Control Committee. Such an arrangement ensures that the SCCC is up and running as soon as the system goes live.

14.5.1 System Change Control

As well as confining changes to the system to the safe and the essential, it is important to effect the change in a cautious and professional manner. The main difficulty is to continue providing a service during and after implementing the change. Even with the best advice and all the deliberations of the SCCC, it is impossible to guarantee that there won't be a hitch when the change is implemented and, even worse, the system does not work as intended with the change successfully made.

In computer systems where maintenance of some level of service is required, there is a security justification for a duplicate set of hardware for administrative and maintenance purposes. Any system change or update should be tested as thoroughly as possible on the duplicate system before it is pressed into service.

From this, it is obvious that the change should be rehearsed. If necessary, this rehearsal should be carried out on the duplicate system as similar as possible to the operational system. Such a facility allows the staff to make several attempts to make the change until they get it right. Secondly, this facility allows the revised configuration to be properly tested before it is inflicted on the user community.

When a change is implemented, it must be reversible should the change turn out to be an operational disaster. Nearly as important as rehearsing the change, it is also wise to ensure that it is possible to revert back to the original configuration with the minimum of delay. Again, this reversion procedure should be rehearsed on the duplicate system before the operational system is updated.

14.6 Database Maintenance

Assuming that the maintenance of a given level of service is a significant part of the system security policy it is important to ensure that any database which forms part of the system is properly maintained. Apart from the database backup policy, already discussed, the maintenance of a database involves the following tasks:

- monitoring the use of the database so that the heavily used and the unused elements can be identified;

- configuring and maintaining the database so that it reflects the current user requirement;
- checking that the database conforms to the current legislation e.g. the Data Protection Act;
- culling redundant elements of the database;
- checking the integrity of the database.

14.6.1 Database Monitoring and Culling

No database can be left to look after itself. If it is allowed to grow in an unmonitored and uncontrolled fashion, it will eventually fill up the available disc space. If the situation is allowed to develop to the state where an update is thwarted due to lack of disc space, the whole integrity of the database may be threatened. At the very least, a lot of time will be lost while the database is restored to a stable and consistent state.

It is important, for a number of reasons, to remove unwanted parts of the database. This implies that, when the database is first specified and designed, provision should be made for the editing and removal of records and, if possible, the addition and removal of fields. By keeping the database itself as compact as possible, the following benefits will accrue:

- removing unused (unwanted) elements of the database will reduce the overall risk of a security breach;
- in general, the smaller the database the better the retrieval performance, especially for searches with complex criteria;
- the smaller the overall database, the shorter the recovery time after a database crash and the easier it will be to maintain a high availability of service, and
- by keeping the database compact, the time and resources required to maintain it will be minimised.

From the viewpoint of performance it is useful to be able to determine which parts of the database are accessed most frequently and which are hardly ever accessed. From this it should be possible to adjust the database configuration to reduce retrieval times to the minimum.

14.6.2 Legal Conformance

Any database which holds the personal details of members of the general public will be subject to legislation such as the UK Data Protection Act. Such legislation normally covers all forms of personal data including medical and financial records. Most of these stipulate conditions and practices for the maintenance of databases containing personal data. These practices are recommended elsewhere in this chapter as highly desirable in the interests of good data security. A fuller discussion of the security aspects of the UK Data Protection Act is found in Chapter 13 of this book.

14.6.3 Database Integrity

Every database should be accompanied by a database checking program. Unless the database is checked regularly, there is a danger that a combination of software errors and operator mistakes will cause inconsistencies to creep into the database. It is important that any such inconsistencies should be detected at the first possible moment for two reasons: firstly, so that the database can be repaired before it becomes badly corrupted and, secondly, the source of the error can be determined and rectified to reduce the likelihood of a repeat of the error.

Because of the vulnerability of the system to such errors, it is essential that a database checking program should be procured for any information system which has any claim to have integrity. When the system is being designed, the requirement for database consistency monitoring should be considered and incorporated into the system. It is far too late to start procuring a checking program when the first anomalies start to show.

The best way to administer a database is to work on a duplicate copy of the database offline. Where possible, the duplicate database should be copied from a 100% system backup. The database maintenance function is another significant justification for the procurement of a duplicate set on hardware for system administration.

14.7 User Account Management

The management of the user accounts is relatively straightforward. The importance of this particular task is that it controls the access and privileges accorded to the various users. Technically, the task could be carried out by almost anybody in the computer manager's staff. However, to implement the function of "user account manager" this way would be highly irresponsible. The task needs to be carried out by a suitably mature and responsible person under the direct supervision of the installation security officer.

The tasks which comprise user account management are:

- the creation of new user accounts;
- the archiving and deletion of accounts no longer required;
- the setting and adjustment of user account privileges;
- the control of user resources such as disc quotas;
- the temporary suspension of user accounts in the absence of the owners; and
- the implementation and maintenance of the password policy.

The mechanics of carrying out these tasks can be assisted by packages such as Sun's `admintool`. Such aids are very useful and, incidentally, assist security by reducing the likelihood of the administrator making silly mistakes.

14.8 Audit Trail Management

Operating systems are apt to generate large quantities of audit records. If nothing is done with these records, eventually the file system will choke with these records. If the audit system is enabled, the audit trail will have to be maintained. This will entail a number of tasks:

- search the audit trail for sequences of events which might represent a security breach;
- weed the audit trail;
- extract any evidence to support an enquiry after a security event;
- archive the audit trail.

These tasks involve considerable effort. There is a temptation for the system administrator to reduce system logging to the barest minimum and to confine weeding and archiving to those occasions when these tasks cannot be put off. In a well-run system, the logging level is determined by the current activities and the currently perceived threat levels. When threat levels are thought to be low, logging can be restricted to the very basics. As the threat levels rise, logging should be enabled for those aspects of the system at risk due to the raised threat levels.

14.9 Summary

This chapter has enumerated a number of administrative tasks essential to the correct functioning of the security aspects of an information system. No technology can supply security that can be installed and left to its own devices. All security requires administering. This administration will almost certainly require the use of a duplicate set of equipment or, at the very least, the dedicated use of the operational hardware out of normal office hours. It is fair to say that the quality of the security of a system is the quality of the administration of the system security.

Chapter 15

The Management of Security

Much of the content of this chapter uses material from an MSc dissertation by Captain Sean Hoag of the Canadian Army written as a part of his UK Army Staff Course studies.

15.1 The Security Management Problem

So far the discussion has been centred mainly on the various techniques one can employ to counter various security threats. Good security consists of rather more than the mere application of countermeasures. It is thought by many people that the answer to any security problem is to apply every available countermeasure. The supposed advantage of this approach is that it covers every eventuality. However, there are a number of difficulties with the indiscriminate approach:

- The expense of using all these countermeasures is likely to be out of all proportion to the threats.
- Not all security techniques are complementary; some countermeasures can actually undermine the effectiveness of others.

An example of how the indiscriminate use of a frequently prescribed security feature can undermine a system security policy is the mechanism which locks out a terminal or user (or both) after 3, say, failed logins. If the main aim of the security policy is the maintenance of a specified level of service then an attacker can use the lock out mechanism to prevent *bona fide* users from getting legitimate access to the system. This can be achieved without the knowledge of any password at all!

Thus, both on the grounds of value for money and effectiveness, the indiscriminate use of security countermeasures is bad security.

The other extreme approach is for a study comprising a detailed analysis of the risks, threats and costs so as to optimise the selection of countermeasures. Although this may eventually result in an ideal solution to the security problem, there are also drawbacks to this approach:

- There are insufficient suitably qualified security specialists to carry out full-blown security studies for every imaginable situation.
- The cost of a full security study may well be of the same order of the costs associated with the risks.
- The time required for a full study will impose costly delays in the completion of the project.
- In many cases, the security situation will actually change during the time the study is carried out.

From this we can deduce that there is no "ideal" procedure to manage the problems posed by the security requirements of an information system. The next section is an attempt to provide an economical logical mechanism to generate an information system security policy.

15.2 A Security Management Methodology

The task of a manager tasked with security responsibilities can be summarised by the following list of tasks:

- firstly, he (or she) has to understand the nature and value of the information system;
- secondly, a detailed assessment has to made of the realistic threats to the information system;
- thirdly, and perhaps the most difficult part, he has to make an estimate of the risks associated with the threats;
- fourthly, from the work carried out, he has to choose the most appropriate security measures and the degree of quality and assurance with which the measures are to be implemented;
- finally, he has to put in place the mechanisms which will ensure that the chosen security measures are implemented and maintained.

The remainder of this chapter consists of a methodology designed to take a non-specialist manager through the necessary stages to implement a set of appropriate security measures.

15.2.1 Knowledge of the Information System

A detailed knowledge of the information system is a prerequisite for any useful security analysis of the system. It may seem unnecessary to mention such an obvious point, but quite often it is an outsider or consultant who is brought in to carry out the analysis. Without such knowledge, any security plan developed from the analysis cannot be particularly pertinent to the information system in question.

This initial investigation should provide answers to the following questions:

- What is the purpose of the information system?
- Who "owns" the system? (i.e., who has the power to change its purpose or close it down?)
- Who provides the data for the system?
- Who uses the information provided by the system?
- What is the value of the information held in the system?
- What is the sensitivity of the information held in the system?
- What are the legal liabilities associated with the system, such as those imposed by the Data Protection Act?
- Who manages the system?

15.2.2 Threat Assessment

The threat assessment is a critical stage in the security analysis process. On the one hand it is important that all the real threats are recognised since one can only develop cost-effective defenses against recognised threats. On the other hand, it is equally important that only realistic threats are allowed for. It can be a very costly business providing defence mechanisms against non-existent threats.

To assist the analyst, there is a list of the most likely threats to an information system in Appendix E. Against each threat are listed the possible appropriate countermeasures. This is intended to reduce the temptation to specify all the fashionable techniques.

15.2.3 Risk Estimation

For every realistic threat, it is necessary to estimate the associated risk. In this context, the term *risk* is defined as the product of the likelihood of the threat actually happening and the "cost" of repairing the resulting damage to the whole system.

From this *risk* figure it is possible to determine what expenditure would be worthwhile to counter such a threat. Unfortunately, in general, there are no convenient tables which can be used to determine the likelihood of a particular event occurring.

15.2.4 Choice of Mechanisms

Having determined what the realistic threats to the information system are and their associated risks, the security manager is in a position to start choosing a cost-effective set of countermeasures. It is suggested that this can be carried out systematically as follows:

- Each threat is assessed on a scale of 0–5: 0 indicating that the threat is irrelevant and 5 indicating deep concern.
- The vulnerability to that particular threat is then assessed from the potential gain from an attack and the likelihood of such an attack being mounted. This results in a vulnerability index value.
- The threat index and the vulnerability index are combined to select the appropriate functionality group for the countermeasures for that threat.

Appendix E consists of a checklist of the most common threats together with some recommended countermeasures.

This procedure should result in strong countermeasures being recommended where very sensitive material is held in a system with many users, and relatively lightweight measures when just private information is held in a system with less than twenty users.

15.3 System Security Policies

Now that the threats have been assessed, the risks estimated and the countermeasures chosen, the manager is now in a position to formulate a security policy. This policy is the foundation for the implementation and maintenance of the chosen security measures. This policy should be expressed as clearly and simply as possible in a document, the SSP document. The UK Government have defined a format suitable for all government associated system security policies.

It is divided into five sections:

1. **Introduction and system overview.** The purpose of this section is to identify the system to which this SSP statement refers. This section should identify the purpose of the information system and the important people and roles associated with the system.
2. **System description.** The purpose of this section is to give a description of the system to which this SSP statement refers. In particular, this section should describe the structure of the system in sufficient detail to show how the system fulfills its role.
3. **Security requirements.** The purpose of this section is to identify and describe all the relevant security threats to the system and the general strategy to be adopted to counter these threats.
4. **The security policy.** The purpose of this section is to describe, in detail, the various countermeasures to be implemented as counters to the threats identified in the previous section.

5. Administration of security. The purpose of this section is to define the responsibilities of the various parties whose duties involve the implementation and maintenance of the security policy defined in this document.

Appendix D is an example of a formal SSP document. The format has been adapted from the format proposed by a British Government security policy technical subcommittee. The value of this format is that it is logical and it covers all security aspects of an IT system without going into undue technical detail.

15.4 Summary

There is a need for a structured approach to the management of information systems security. Such an approach should, as far as possible, eliminate emotion and prejudice from the identification of threats and the creation of a security policy.

1. There needs to be an investigation into the information system (in the widest sense, not just the technological part) so that it, and its purpose, is correctly understood. This may involve the use of *soft systems*.
2. Once the system is understood, the threats to the system should be identified.
3. For each threat, the associated risks must be estimated.
4. From this, an appropriate set of countermeasures can be drawn up and prioritised.
5. The system security policy document can be written.

This security policy document, once agreed to by the manager of the organisation, should form the basis of all subsequent security activity.

Chapter 16

Conclusions

In the introduction to this book, it was stated that the aim of this book was to provide answers to five questions:

- What is security?
- What are the security problems particular to an IT system?
- What can be done to reduce the security risks associated with such a system?
- In a given situation, what are the appropriate security countermeasures?
- How should one set about procuring an information system with security implications?

As with all interesting problems, there are no simple answers to these basic questions. This chapter will attempt to provide some simplified answers to these questions supported by arguments elsewhere in this book.

Before answering these questions, it will be useful to remind you of the players involved with the security of an information system. These players are:

- the management;
- the workers;
- the implementors and maintainers; and
- the "experts".

Of these, in the implementation of security, the managers and the workers are the most important. The implementors and maintainers are neutral in security matters. On the positive side, they should provide a secure system and the means to run it. On the negative side, hired programmers and engineers can pose a security threat. The role of the "experts" is to act as advisers; for management to employ the "experts" to implement security is irresponsible and a misuse of a valuable resource.

16.1 A Definition of Information System Security

One plausible definition of security might be:

> Security is the means whereby management maintains the mechanisms which allow the efficient and economic conduct of the business of the enterprise.

When applied to information systems, this definition encompasses the availability, integrity and exclusivity aspects of information security. It also stresses the involvement of management in the security process.

16.2 The Security Problems of an Information System

In many ways the security issues associated with an information system are very similar to those in a traditional paper-based system. What differences there are, are mostly differences of emphasis. The introduction of new technologies has made little difference to the classical security precautions: physical security, personnel security and procedural security. The introduction of new technologies has opened up new lines of attack and new vulnerabilities for information systems. The two most important differences resulting from the introduction of computer technology are:

- In the matter of personnel security, very few organisations can afford to employ suitably trained staff to handle all the possible technological problems that can arise in an information system. Consequently, there is a need to employ outside contractors who will, inevitably, have access to the most sensitive aspects of an enterprise.
- In the matter of technological threats, it is important to consider the security implications at the very earliest stages of the procurement process so that as many as possible of the technical vulnerabilities can be designed out of the system.

The main purpose of any security measure is to reduce the risk of a security incident ever happening and minimising the negative consequences of an actual security incident. Individual security measures can be breached; consequently, it is unwise to rely on just one blockbuster security feature. Security measures should be chosen so that they defend the system in depth in such a way that the breach of any single measure should not leave the rest of the system vulnerable.

It is worth closing this section with a sobering thought: the designers of secure systems tend to concentrate on those aspects of security they know about and give scant thought as to what a real attacker would be likely to do.

16.3 Tailpiece

Security runs smoothly and efficiently when it is run by management who consult security experts. Security is rarely successful when management delegates the running of security to the experts.

Appendix A

Unix Security Resources

It is complex and tedious to check a Unix (or Linux) system for anomolies. Fortunately many good people out there have done a lot of the work to take the backache out of the checking. There are several well known packages, many of them free, available for use in the support of Unix systems. There are far fewer equivalent security resources available for Windows NT, mainly because Windows NT has not been around for so long and the design and source code for Windows NT are not in the public domain.

There are several different types of security resource:

- software tools to check for the safe and secure configuration of a Unix system;
- software tools which monitor local area network activity;
- software tools to detect intruders in a system;
- software tools to check for changes to the system configuration;
- software tools to check for sensible passwords;
- firewall software;
- secure operating systems and applications software;
- documentation.

These various categories are considered in turn below. The list of packages discussed is not intended to be comprehensive. The examples quoted are to give the reader a flavour of the types of tools available in early 2001. Most of these tools are still undergoing development; it is beyond the scope of a book such as this to provide a comprehensive and up to date catalogue of software security tools. It must be said that just because a particular tool is not mentioned in this list is no reflection on the quality or usefulness of that tool. The packages mentioned are a mixture of proprietary and open source. The proprietary packages need to be purchased and may cost a lot of money; however, in general, they are better documented and simpler to configure correctly. Some of the open source packages may have better functionality but may need very special expertise to configure properly.

A.1 Configuration Checkers

The two main packages are COPS and TIGER. COPS stands for the Computer Oracle and Password System. TIGER is produced as part of a set of security tools by Texas A&M University. They both consist of a fairly comprehensive set of scripts which will check a host for known vulnerabilities. Each contain a number of shell scripts and programs. The major areas of checking are:

- cron entries are checked.
- mail aliases are checked.
- NFS exports are checked.
- inetd entries are checked so that only the required services are enabled.
- PATH variables are checked.
- .rhosts and .netrc files are checked.
- Specific file and directory access permissions are checked.
- File system scans to locate unusual files.
- Digital signatures are used to detect alterations to key binaries (signatures are generated from CD-ROM) and also to report binaries for which (updated) security patches exist.
- Pathnames embedded in any files reported by most of the other checks are checked.

These checks cover most of the known areas of vulnerabilities. A full check of a computer system typically takes about 1 hour. In addition COPS employs a version of the "Crack" package to check the system for weak passwords. TIGER includes a tigercron utility which can run individual checks at suitable intervals and at convenient times of day. TIGER and other related packages can be had from:

    http://net.tamu.edu/pub/network/public.html

and COPS for Linux can be had from:

    ftp://ftp.freebsd.org/pub/FreeBSD/ports/i386/\
        packages-4-release/All/cops-1.04.tgz

A.2 Network Activity Monitors

Network activity monitors are a useful aid to understanding what is going on within a local area network. There are general surveyance programs such as

"Angel" (http://www.MPA-Garching.MPG.DE/angel) which give a coloured
tote board display of the current network activity and "Ethereal" which can
be used for very detailed analysis of every packet on the local area network.
This type of tool is likely to be of more use with relatively large corporate
networks where there is greater likelihood of locally originated mischief.

A.3 Intrusion Checkers

The Network ICE Corporation (http://www.networkice.com) produce a
proprietary package called "BlackICE Defender" which can detect any attempt by an outsider to probe a computer running Windows95/98/NT/2000.
It claims to be able to trace the source of any probe and to record all attempted transactions by the potential attacker in a form which can be used in
any subsequent investigation or court proceedings. It appears to be a useful
defence tool for an isolated Internet user who is not protected by a corporate firewall system. It would appear to be some protection from a speculative
hacker. However, it cannot prevent the importing of worms and viruses transmitted via the Internet (e.g., by e-mail).

A.4 Change Detectors

Change detector packages are configured with a list of system files which
should not be altered in the normal course of events. The hypothesis is that
any change to such files could have only occurred as a result of some form
of attack. When the system is set up, MD5 sumchecks of the protected files
are held in a database, itself protected by an MD5 sumcheck. Periodically,
the package scans the protected files recalculating the sumchecks. The new
sumcheck is compared to the original version. Any discrepancies found act
as evidence that an attack may have taken place. Recovery is effected by
overwriting the disturbed files with copies of the backed up originals.

When a system upgrade takes place, the change detector system needs to
be disabled and the sumchecks recalculated once the upgrade is complete.

There are a number of such packages. Most of this functionality is incorporated into the COPS package. "Tripwire" is perhaps the most widely
known change detector package. There are versions which run on most variants of Unix and Windows NT. Tripwire has more useful features than those
described above. In the configuration database, there is provision for more
detailed monitoring of certain classes of files such as system log files which
are allowed to grow and the detailed recording of file attributes. From the
administrative point of view, Tripwire has a built-in configurable report generator which considerably reduces the manual overheads of maintaining the
system. "Tripwire" is obtainable from: http://www.tripwiresecurity.com.

A.5 Password Checkers

Satan and Crack are password cracking packages. Currently, both use the DES derived Unix password encryption algorithm. Apparently, there are plans to introduce MD5 versions in the near future. Both packages are based around highly optimised encryption algorithms and can perform tens of thousands of password encryptions per minute. Using modern computer hardware (e.g., Intel PIII 500MHz) they are capable of scanning a site's password list with about 2500 entries in about 3 hours. They use an intelligent brute force approach. For each password entry, they try a set of guesses based around the user's name and other details recorded in the password file entry. They follow by systematically going through the system dictionary and locally configured dictionaries. The results of each encryption is compared to the encrypted passwords held in the password file. When a match is found, the password is broken. The results of such a scan should be used by management to persuade users to choose better passwords.

More information about Satan can be obtained from:

```
ftp://ftp.mcs.anl.gov/pub/security
```

Crack is freely available on most major academic software mirrors e.g.,

```
http://sunsite.org.uk/public/packages/\
    FreeBSD/FreeBSD-stable/ports/security/crack
```

A.6 Firewall Packages

There are a number of firewall packages about. The most famous must be "Gauntlet" from PGP International. This is a high quality proprietary product available for Windows NT as well as Solaris and HP-UX. For more details try:

```
http://www.pgp.com/products/gauntlet/default.asp
```

There are several open source and shareware firewall kits available. The main disadvantage of these is that they require considerable expertise to set up and configure correctly. Further, the degree of support required to sustain the required level of service may not always be available.

Gauntlet would appear to have an additional advantage over the other (open source) firewall packages in that it claims to have virus scanning software built into the packet filtering mechanism. This would reduce the chances of a successful worm attack on the defended local area network.

A.7 Security Documentation

It is important to keep up to date in respect of security problems and appropriate countermeasures. The Internet is by far the most convenient medium for keeping up to date. The main source of information has to be the CERT web site:

    http://www.cert.org

This source of information is supplemented by a number of other sites:

L0pht Heavy Industries	`http://www.10pht.com/advisories.html`
Computer Associates	`http://www.cai.com/virusinfo/encyclopedia`
NIH Computer Security Information	`http://www.alw.nih.gov/Security`

A.8 Other Secure Software

As well as the general tools listed in this section, it is possible to procure special versions of operating systems such as Solaris (Sun Unix), SCO Unix and Windows NT. These "secure" versions of the operating systems have some functionality removed, where that is thought to improve security. There may be some additional functionality, particularly in the matter of the control of access to files and physical peripheral devices. These "secure" versions of the software will have undergone additional testing so as to ensure that known security holes have been eliminated. There is a limited market for such software so the licence fees will be several times that for the normal versions of the software.

There is a second disadvantage to such software. Because of the comparatively limited user base, there may be several latent errors still waiting to be encountered and reported by the users. It is still a matter of speculation whether the additional testing is sufficient to compensate for the relative lack of exposure to real users.

The list below consists of commercially available "secure" (assurance level E3) database products taken from old (1998) sales information. There may be newer more up-to-date versions available in 2001. There is no guarantee that these particular versions of these products are any more reliable than the equivalent unassured versions.

CA-Open Ingres/Enhanced Security Rel 1.1	Computer Associates
Informix-Online V7.23	Informix Software Ltd
Trusted Oracle 7	Oracle Corporation

Appendix B

DoD Computer System Evaluation Criteria

The Orange Book lays down some 27 properties of secure computer systems which required assessment and defined 7 levels of assurance. The list of security properties is very complete and comprises the following:

Audit. The Trusted Computer Base (TCB) shall be able to create, maintain and protect from modification an audit trail of all accesses or attempted accesses of any object that the TCB protects. The scale of auditing is dependent on the actual assurance level.

Configuration management. At assurance levels B and A, there is a requirement to maintain a configuration management regime both during the development of the system and, for level A1, during the entire life cycle of the system. The configuration management requirements are particularly detailed for the TCB, less so for the rest of the software.

Covert channel analysis. The system developer is required to make a detailed analysis of the system searching for covert channels and to measure or estimate the bandwidth of any channel found.

Design documentation. The designer is required to make available documentation that describes the supplier's protection philosophy and how this is implemented in the TCB. At the higher assurance levels, there is less emphasis on *description* and more on *proof*.

Design specification and verification. A model of the security policy supported by the TCB shall be maintained over the life cycle of the ADP system and demonstrated (and *proved* for assurance levels B2 and above) to be consistent with its axioms.

Device labels. The TCB shall support the assignment of minimum and maximum security levels to all physically attached devices. These security levels are to be used by the TCB to enforce the local security policy.

Discretionary access control. The TCB shall define and control access between named users and named objects (e.g., files, programs and physical devices) in the system. The TCB is to enforce user specified self/group/public sharing of user owned objects.

Exporting of labelled information. The TCB shall designate each I/O device and communication channel as either single-level or multi-level. Any changes must be effected manually and must be audited.

Exportation of multi-level devices. When the TCB exports an object to a multi-level I/O device, the sensitivity label associated with that object shall be exported to, and reside on, the same physical medium as the exported information.

Exportation to single-level devices. Single-level I/O devices are not required to maintain the sensitivity labels of the information they process. However the TCB must contain a reliable mechanism, with audit, which enables an authorised user to designate the single security level to be associated with that particular device.

Identification and authentication. The TCB shall require users to identify themselves to it at the beginning of any interactive session and the TCB shall use a protected mechanism (e.g., passwords) to authenticate the user's identity. The TCB is to protect the authentication mechanism from unauthorised access. The TCB is to use the authenticated user identity to associate any auditable action with the user attempting it.

Label integrity. Sensitivity labels shall accurately represent the security levels of the subjects or objects with which they are associated.

Labelling human readable output. The TCB shall mark the beginning and end of all human readable, paged, hard copy or screen output with human readable sensitivity labels that properly represent the sensitivity of the output. Any override of this sensitivity marking shall be auditable.

Labels. Sensitivity labels associated with all subjects and objects under its control shall be maintained by the TCB.

Mandatory access control. The TCB shall enforce a mandatory access control policy over all subjects and storage objects under its control. All such subjects and objects shall be assigned sensitivity labels. The TCB shall be able to support two or more such security levels. The enforced security policy is to conform to the Bell and LaPadula model.

Object reuse. All authorisations to the information contained within a storage object shall be revoked prior to initial assignment, allocation or reallocation to a subject from the TCBs pool of unused storage objects. No information produced by a prior subject's actions is to be made available to any subject that obtains access to an object that has been released back to the system.

Security features guide. There shall be a user document which describes the protection mechanisms provided by the TCB, gives guidelines as to their use, and indicates how they interact with each other.

Security testing . The security mechanisms of the ADP system shall be tested so as to demonstrate that the implementation conforms to the high level specification. As the assurance level increases so does the formality of the testing.

Subject sensitivity labels. The TCB shall immediately notify a terminal user of each change in the security level associated with that user during an interactive session. A terminal user shall be able to query the TCB at any time for a display of the subject's complete sensitivity label.

System architecture. The TCB shall maintain a domain for its own execution that protects it from external interference or tampering. Resources controlled by the TCB are a defined subset of the ADP system and should be subject to all access control and audit mechanisms.

System integrity. The system must include hardware/software facilities that can be used to validate the correct functioning of the hardware and firmware aspects of the TCB.

Test documentation. The system developer shall supply the system evaluators with a document that describes the test plan, the test procedures that show how the security features were tested, and the results of the security mechanisms' functional testing.

Trusted distribution. A trusted ADP system control and distribution facility shall be provided for the integrity of the mapping between the master up-to-date version of the TCB and the on-site master copy of the code for the current version (applicable only to assurance level A1).

Trusted facility management. The TCB shall support separate operator and administrator functions. The functions performed in the role of security administrator shall be identified. The ADP system administrative personnel shall only be able to carry out administrator functions after performing a distinct auditable action to assume the security administrator role. Non-security functions that can be performed in this role shall be limited strictly to those essential to the effective performance of the security administrators role.

Trusted facility manual. There shall be a manual addressed to the ADP system administrator describing the administrative facilities provided for the security administration of the system. This document should contain cautions about the functions and privileges that should be controlled when running a secure facility.

Trusted path. The TCB should support a trusted communications path between itself and the user for initial login and authentication. Communications via this path shall be initiated exclusively by the user. In a multilevel environment, a trusted communications path shall be used whenever a *positive TCB to user* connection is required (e.g., login, change of subject security level, change of object security level etc.). All communications via such a path should be logically isolated and unmistakenly distinguishable from all other paths.

Trusted recovery: consists of the provision of procedures and/or mechanisms such that recovery after a system failure is achieved without a security compromise.

The most important aspect of the Orange Book lies in the definition of the 7 levels of assurance. These assurance levels are listed below in ascending order of strictness; each level subsumes the features of all previous levels.

D   **Minimal protection** with no special security features at all; e.g., a personal computer in an unlocked room.

C1   **Discretionary access control.** The system requires a login/password authentication procedure and must provide protections based on ownership or role for data and the use of facilities; e.g., the Unix operating system. This class of environment is expected to be used by cooperating users processing data at the same level of sensitivity.

C2   **Controlled access protection.** Systems in this class enforce a more finely grained discretionary access control than C1 systems. Users are now individually accountable for their actions through login procedures, stricter resource management and the auditing of security related events. Operating system environments such as DEC VMS conform to this level of assurance; particular issues (e.g., V4.7) were formally validated to this level.

B1   **Labelled security protection.** Class B1 systems require all the features required for class C2 with the addition of an informal statement of the security policy model. Data labelling and mandatory access controls over named subjects and objects must be implemented and any exported objects must be correctly labelled. All errors shown up in the course of the testing of the security features must be corrected. There are a number of special versions of proprietary operating systems which comply with this standard.

B2   **Structured protection.** In class B2 systems, the TCB is based on a clearly defined and documented formal security policy model that requires the discretionary and mandatory access control enforcement found in class B1 systems to be extended to all the subjects and objects in the computer system. The additional features at this level include dealing with the *covert channel*[1] problem, the strengthening of the authentication mechanisms and the provision of trusted facility management for the system management personnel. The TCB has to be carefully structured so as to simplify its testing and verification. The system should be reasonably "hacker proof". The hardware and software components of the TCB are subject to strict configuration management procedures.

---

[1] A *covert channel* is a communication channel that allows a process to transfer information in a way that violates the system's security policy. There are two

B3   **Security domains**. Class B3 systems are functionally similar to class B2 systems with new facilities for the auditing and signalling of security related events, the clean and safe recovery of data after a system crash and the provision of facilities to support the role of a system security administrator which is entirely independent of the computer system administration. There are constraints on the complexity and size of the TCB as all the critical elements of the TCB are now subject to close scrutiny. The system itself should be "tamper-proof" and should be highly resistant to hacking.

A1   **Verified design**. An A1 system is functionally equivalent to a B3 system. The difference lies in the care taken in the specification, design and implementation of the system so that there is a high degree of confidence that the conformance of the implementation to the formal top level specification can be validated for every stage in the production process of the system. The implementation process will almost certainly require the use of mathematically formal methods such as Z and static analysis (MALPAS). Currently, there are no systems available at this level.

A few specially redesigned versions of particular proprietary operating systems have been validated to the B2 level of assurance.

---

varieties of covert channel: a covert storage channel which makes use of a block of storage shared by two subjects at different security levels, and covert timing channels which convey information by the modulation of a system resource (e.g., CPU time) in such a way that it affects some phenomenon observable by a second subject (e.g., system response time).

	A1	B3	B2	B1	C2	C1	D
Audit	4	4	3	2	1		
Configuration Management	2	2	1				
Covert Channel Analysis	3	2	1				
Design Documentation	5	4	3	2	1	1	
Design Specification and Verification	4	3	2	1			
Device Labels	1	1	1				
Discretionary Access Control	3	3	2	2	2	1	
Exportation of Labelled Information	1	1	1	1			
Exportation to Multi-Level Devices	1	1	1	1			
Exportation to Single-Level Devices	1	1	1	1			
Identification and Authentication	3	3	3	3	2	1	
Label Integrity	1	1	1	1			
Labelling Human Readable Output	1	1	1	1			
Labels	2	2	2	1			
Mandatory Access Control	2	2	2	1			
Object Reuse	1	1	1	1	1		
Security Features User's Guide	1	1	1	1	1	1	
Security Testing	6	5	4	3	2	1	
Subject Sensitivity Labels	1	1	1				
System Architecture	5	5	4	3	2	1	
System Integrity	1	1	1	1	1	1	
Test Documentation	3	2	2	1	1	1	
Trusted Distribution	1						
Trusted Facility Management	2	2	1				
Trusted Facility Manual	5	5	4	3	2	1	
Trusted Path	2	2	1				
Trusted Recovery	1	1					

Fig. B.1: The Orange Book trusted computer system evaluation criteria summary chart. (The numbers indicate the required degree of functionality at each level.)

Appendix C

IT Security Evaluation Criteria (ITSEC)

The 1991 ITSEC document is a more flexible refinement of the DoD Orange Book. It differs from the Orange Book in two important respects:

- It suggests that security features can be selected in more flexible combinations than those defined in the Orange Book.
- It separates the security functionalities from the assurance criteria. Consequently it is possible to specify a relatively low level of security functionality but insist that the system is implemented to a relatively high degree of assurance. This flexibility makes the concept of secure software systems rather more attractive to the commercial world.

The ITSEC document proposes about ten standard functionality classes:

F-C1: This class provides discretionary (need-to-know) access control and is derived from the Orange Book class C1.

F-C2: This class provides a more finely grained discretionary access control and introduces the auditing of some security related events. This class is derived from the Orange Book class C2.

F-B1: This class defines sensitivity labels and provides basic facilities for the enforcement of mandatory access control. This class is derived from the Orange Book class B1.

F-B2: This class extends mandatory access control to all subjects and objects and is a general strengthening of F-B1. This class is derived from the Orange Book class B2.

F-B3: This class provides for the separation of the roles of security administration and computer administration, and auditing is expanded to cover all security related events. This class is derived from the Orange Book classes B3 and A1.

F-IN: This class defines the functionality appropriate for systems with high integrity requirements for programs and data.

F-AV: This class defines the functionality appropriate for systems with high availability requirements.

F-DI: This class defines the functionality appropriate for the safeguarding of data integrity during data exchange.

F-DC: This class defines the functionality appropriate for the safeguarding of data confidentiality during data exchange. (A cryptographic system is a possible candidate for this class.)

F-DX: This class defines the functionality appropriate for networks with demanding requirements for both confidentiality and integrity.

In addition to specifying the functionalities of secure systems, the ITSEC document specifies three sets of specification languages for secure systems: an *informal* specification language, some acceptable *semi-formal* specification languages and some *formal* specification languages.

The ITSEC document specifies that an *informal specification* is written in natural language (e.g., English) rather than a notation requiring special restrictions or conventions. It goes on to say that a natural language specification shall be written with the aim of minimising ambiguity by ensuring that all terms are used consistently and ensuring that any term with a specialised meaning defined in a glossary of terms.

A *semi-formal* style of specification requires the use of some restricted notation according to a set of conventions referenced by the specification. A semi-formal style can be graphical and/or based on the restricted use of natural language, for example, data-flow diagrams, state transition diagrams and entity-relationship diagrams. It goes on to state that structured design and development methods normally incorporate such a semi-formal style. As examples it mentions the Yourden Structured Method, Structured Analysis and Design Technique (SADT), Structured Systems Analysis and Design Method (SSADM) and Jackson Structured Design. It ends by recommending the Claims language which is defined in Annex B of the ITSEC document.

Under *formal specifications* it recommends the use of one of VDM, Z, RAISE and Gypsy.

The ITSEC document lists five possible formal security models:

The Bell and LaPadula model [1] which is suitable for the specification of national mandatory access control requirements.

The Clark and Wilson model [4] which is suitable for the specification of the integrity requirements of commercial transaction processing systems.

The Brewer–Nash model [3] which is suitable for the specification of the access control requirements for client confidentiality in a financial services institution.

The Eizenberg model [8] which is suitable for the specification of access control rights which vary with time.

The Landwehr model [22] which is suitable for the specification of the data exchange requirements of a data network.

It is one thing to specify the functionality of a computer system; it is quite another matter to have full confidence in the manner and the extent to which a system implements these functional requirements. At one extreme, if one accepts the supplier's assertions and the contents of the user documentation, one has a relatively low level of assurance (confidence) in the quality of the software. However, this naive approach has the advantage of being relatively cheap. At the other extreme, if a very high degree of assurance is required, it can cost more than the original system implementation costs to determine how fully it implements the original specifications. The ITSEC document specifies six levels of assurance so that it is possible to choose different balances between acquisition costs and assurance costs to suit different circumstances. These six levels of assurance are summarised in the tables below: as the levels of assurance increase, the requirements assume the requirements of all the lower levels of assurance.

Table C.1: Level E1 assurance summary

Specification	Rationale, list of security enforcing functions specified informally, the SSP
Architecture	The general structure of the ToE with a statement of the hardware/firmware protection mechanisms
Detailed Design	*No requirement*
Implementation	Test documentation showing the plan, purpose, procedures and results of the tests.
Development	
Configuration Control	The configuration list identifying the version of the ToE and how the ToE is uniquely identified.
Programming Language	*No requirement*
Developers' Security	*No requirement*
Operational Documentation	Provide user documentation and administrative documentation.
User Documentation	Should state how a user uses the ToE in a secure manner.
Administrative Documentation	Should state how the ToE is administered in a secure manner.
Delivery and Installation	A statement of how various configurations affect security.
Operation	Should provide procedures for the secure start-up and operation of the ToE.

The E1 assurance level is the basic assurance entry level and is roughly equivalent to the assurance levels specified for level C1 in the DoD Orange Book.

Table C.2: Level E2 assurance summary

Specification	Rationale, list of security enforcing functions specified informally, the SSP
Architecture	The general structure of the ToE with a statement of the hardware/firmware protection mechanisms. It should separate the ToE into security enforcing mechanisms and other components.
Detailed Design	Shall identify and describe all the security enforcement mechanisms, components and their interfaces.
Implementation	Shall include a full regression testing system.
Development	Shall be carried out with programming development tools within a configuration control system.
Configuration Control	*Essentially as for E1.*
Programming Language	*No requirement*
Developers' Security	Shall state the measures and the environment to protect the integrity of the ToE under development.
Operational Documentation	Provide user documentation and administrative documentation.
User Documentation	Should state how a user uses the ToE in a secure manner.
Administrative Documentation	Should state how the ToE is administered in a secure manner.
Delivery and Installation	The procedures should guarantee the authenticity of the delivered ToE.
Operation	The start up procedures should contain code to test and verify any security enforcement components and mechanisms.

The E2 assurance level is the assurance level normally expected to be found in validated, basically "secure", versions of such operating systems as Unix, such as Solaris with security options. It is roughly equivalent to the assurance levels specified for level C2 in the DoD Orange Book.

Table C.3: Level E3 assurance summary

Specification	Rationale, list of security enforcing functions specified informally, the SSP
Architecture	The general structure of the ToE with a statement of the hardware/firmware protection mechanisms. It should separate the ToE into security enforcing mechanisms and other components.
Detailed Design	The design shall specify all basic components. It shall identify and describe all the security enforcement mechanisms, components and their interfaces.
Implementation	Over and above the requirements of level E2, the correspondence between sections of source code (or machine drawings) and the basic components of the detailed design.
Development	The documentation should include details of the internal acceptance procedures and a list of all the implementation programming languages used.
Configuration Control	As for level E2 plus all procedure definitions, source code and drawings should carry unique version markings.
Programming Language	Any programming language used for implementation shall be well defined e.g., as an ISO standard. Any language implementation dependent features used shall be documented.
Developers' Security	*Essentially as for E2.*
Operational Documentation	*Essentially as for E2.*
User Documentation	*Essentially as for E2.*
Administrative Documentation	*Essentially as for E2.*
Delivery and Installation	*Essentially as for E2.*
Operation	*Essentially as for E2.*

The E3 assurance level is the assurance level normally expected to be found in validated medium "secure" versions of an operating system. It is roughly equivalent to the assurance levels specified for level B1 in the DoD Orange Book.

Table C.4: Level E4 assurance summary

Specification	As for level E3 but with a formal security policy model and an informal interpretation of the model as applied to this implementation.
Architecture	The design is to be expressed in terms of a semi-formal notation.
Detailed Design	The semi-formal notation shall be carried through to the detailed design of all the security enforcing components.
Implementation	The test plan shall include a justification that the test coverage is sufficient (e.g. all paths through security enforcing components are covered).
Development	An audit mechanism shall be implemented on the configuration control keeping track of all modifications to the ToE.
Configuration Control	Procedures shall be implemented which only allow changes to the ToE to be carried out by authorised personnel.
Programming Language	As for level E3 plus full documentation of any compilation options used.
Developers' Security	*Essentially as for E2.*
Operational Documentation	*Essentially as for E2.*
User Documentation	*Essentially as for E2.*
Administrative Documentation	*Essentially as for E2.*
Delivery and Installation	*Essentially as for E2.*
Operation	*Essentially as for E2.*

The E4 assurance level is rarely found as it falls between the two most popular assurance levels: E3 and E5. It is roughly equivalent to the assurance levels specified for level B2 in the DoD Orange Book.

Table C.5: Level E5 assurance summary

Specification	Essentially as for E4.
Architecture	As for level E4 plus a requirement for fuller explanations of system interfaces in a semi-formal language.
Detailed Design	As for level E4 plus a requirement of a full separation of the security enforcing mechanisms. All unnecessary functionality shall be excluded from the security enforcing mechanisms. All variables common to more than one module shall be identified and explained. Full use should be made of functional layering, abstraction and data hiding.
Implementation	As for level E4 plus a requirement that the source code and hardware drawings should be completely structured into small comprehensible separate sections. These should define their correspondence with the appropriate unit(s) of the detailed design.
Development	As for level E4 plus a full definition of the integration procedure and the source code of all library routines used.
Configuration Control	Full configuration control is to be implemented: all objects created shall be subject to configuration control; the person responsible for the acceptance of a unit shall not be one of its implementors or designers. All security relevant objects shall be identified as such; those other objects affected by such a change should be readily identifiable.
Programming Language	As for level E4 plus the availability of the source code of all libraries used.
Developers' Security	Essentially as for E2 with more emphasis on the full explanation of the security procedures associated with the ToE development.
Operational Documentation	Essentially as for E2.
User Documentation	Essentially as for E2.
Administrative Documentation	Essentially as for E2.
Delivery and Installation	Essentially as for E2.
Operation	Essentially as for E2.

The E5 assurance level is the assurance level normally expected to be found in validated most "secure" versions of an operating system. It is roughly equivalent to the assurance levels specified for level B3 in the DoD Orange Book.

Table C.6: Level E6 assurance summary

Specification	As for level E5 plus the formal specification of security enforcing functions and the requirement for a library of test programs and tools which can be used to detect any inconsistencies between source code and the corresponding executable code (e.g. a disassembler and/or debugger).
Architecture	As for level E5 plus a requirement to demonstrate the conformance of the design with the underlying formal security policy using a combination of formal and informal techniques.
Detailed Design	Essentially as for E5.
Implementation	As for level E5 plus the requirement to explain the correspondence of the implementation of the security enforcing mechanisms at the source code level to the formal specification of the security enforcing functions of the ToE.
Development	Essentially as for E5.
Configuration Control	As for level E5 plus the requirement that all tools used in the development process shall be subject to configuration control.
Programming Language	Essentially as for E5.
Developers' Security	Essentially as for E5.
Operational Documentation	Essentially as for E2.
User Documentation	Essentially as for E2.
Administrative Documentation	Essentially as for E2.
Delivery and Installation	As for level E2 plus the requirement that if different configurations are possible, they shall be defined in terms of the formal architectural design and the impact of the configuration on security shall be explained.
Operation	Essentially as for E2.

The E6 assurance level is the highest assurance level specified in the IT-SEC document and is approximately equivalent to the assurance levels specified for level A1 in the DoD —Orange Book. This level is extremely rigorous and very expensive to implement in full. Consequently there are very few software systems validated to this level of assurance.

Appendix D

An Example System Security Policy

This example is based very loosely on one of the UK MoD policy document structures. It has been abbreviated and simplified so as to be more generally useful. This example is intended to be fairly complete, in fact, some would say exaggerated. In this example, there is a fairly complete list of headings so as to act as an aide mémoire for anyone drawing up a policy document based on this example. In any practical example, it is only necessary to include those subsections deemed to be relevant. The business described is entirely fictitious and any resemblance to any actual enterprise is purely coincidental.

1   Introduction and System Overview

(The purpose of this section is to identify the actual system to which this SSP statement refers.)

1.1   Scope of this Document

This document represents the consolidated statement of security policy for the computer network in the J.R. Whitman Ltd., hardware stores, of Dinklebury, Gloucestershire and in the branches in Dursley and Painswick.

1.2   Name of the System

The computer network together with its associated computers is collectively known as *Bookkeeper*.

1.3   Users of the System

Bookkeeper is used by the management and staff of J.R. Whitman Ltd.
These consist of the proprietor, Mr James Whitman, his two sons, David
and George, the three branch managers, the head bookkeeper and eight full-
time and part time-sales staff.

1.4   Timescales and Milestones

The *Bookkeeper* system was brought into service 1st March 1996. The aim
of this security policy document is to review security in the current system
and to ensure any improvements are implemented and in service by 1st June
1998.

1.5   Project Security Advisors and Auditors

PK Management Plc. are the suppliers of the main software packages used by
the business. They have designed and implemented a range of software packages for use by small businesses. They have provided advice for the selection
and configuration of packages for J.R. Whitman Ltd.

Grunt Thornbush & Partners are the business auditors; as such, they have
a brief to ensure that the business practices are not susceptible to fraud or
abuse. In this role, they should advise on the accounting system to be used
and how it should be implemented.

2   System Description

(The purpose of this section is to give a reasonably detailed description of the actual system.)

2.1   Role of the System

The *Bookkeeper* system performs all the administrative support for a small rural hardware retail chain. The main components of *Bookkeeper* are:

- the main accounts ledger;
- the business payroll;
- the stock ledger;
- point-of-sale support.

These four main functional areas interact. Should any one of these functions fail for any length of time, it would be very difficult to sustain the business.

2.2   System Architecture

The *Bookkeeper* system consists of five PCs: one for the accounts ledger and payroll systems, a second for the stock ledger system and the remaining three provide point-of-sale support at each of the three premises. There is a sixth, stand alone machine at the Dinklebury premises used for word processing and correspondence.

The three branches are interconnected by modems and dial–up lines. Normally, the Dursley and Painswick point-of-sale support machines work in stand-alone mode. However, every evening they are connected to the main stock ledger machine at Dinklebury so as to exchange information. At very busy times, the machine may be also connected during the lunch hour. The Dinklebury point-of-sale support machine is permanently connected to the stock ledger machine. The three point-of-sale machines are essentially identical and are interchangeable.

All networked machines are protected by Uninterruptable Power Supplies (UPS) which can keep the computers going for up to 30 minutes without mains power. Should a power cut last longer than 20 minutes at the Dinklebury premises, there is a Honda 2.5 Kva portable generator which can be used to power the local point-of-sale machine and the stock control system so that the business can continue to trade.

All computers are covered by a 4 hour response maintenance contract with Safe Systems Plc. of Bristol. Normally, a Safe System's engineer is on site within two hours of a call out.

2.3   The Global Security Environment (GSE)

The GSE, in Dinklebury, Dursley and Painswick, consists of the surroundings
of the premises. In all three cases, the shop fronts open out onto the pavement in the shopping area. Law and order is the responsibility of the Chief
Constable, Gloucestershire County Constabulary. Due to funding constraints,
the local police do not provide regular foot patrols. Response to "999" calls
is variable, typically 10–15 minutes, provided resources can be found in the
South Gloucestershire Division. In Dinklebury, several small businesses have
clubbed together to hire the services of Square Deal Security Services, who
provide a regular patrol of all subscribing business premises out of normal
trading hours. The duties of the Square Deal patrolmen are: to check the
security of premises and to look for signs of suspicious activity, and to call
the police and notify the owner of the premises should circumstances warrant
it. The duties of the patrolmen do not extend to direct physical intervention,
even when intruders are caught red-handed.

During normal business hours, the GSE extends to the shop retail trading
areas as described below. The retail area is where the shops' display goods
are located. Customers are encouraged to circulate around the retail area to
view and handle the goods on display. When a customer selects an item that
he or she wishes to buy, he or she takes the item to a cash till where the
purchase can be effected.

Customers are normally confined to the retail area. The layout of the
retail area is such that all of it can be observed by staff either directly from
the till area or indirectly through mirrors or closed circuit television.

2.4   The Local Security Environment (LSE)

The LSE for each site consists of a cash till area, a stock room and an office
area. The actual layouts at the three sites are all different; however, the same
principles are applied to each site.

The till area is separated from the retail area by a counter. Tills and
receipt books are kept behind the counter. The counter is also the first line
of physical defence for the stock rooms and offices as the doors through to
the "back of the shop" are all positioned behind the counter.

In general, these premises are considered to be low risk: there are never
large amounts of cash held on the premises and none of the normal stock
items are of high value. If a customer wishes to purchase a high value item,
this will be ordered specially.

2.5   The Electronic Security Environment (ESE)

The ESE consists of the the computer systems, the tills and the bar code
readers. Physically, these items are kept in areas where access is restricted to
the employees of J.R. Whitman Ltd.

3   Security Requirements

(This section describes the required security features to be incorporated into the system.)

3.1   Vulnerabilities

The most valuable information assets of *Bookkeeper* consist of the financial records on the accounts ledger system and the stock records on the stock ledger system. If this data were to be lost, it would severely impede the conduct of day-to-day business.

The next in order of priority is the correspondence on the word processing machine. Loss of this correspondence would be a great embarrassment to the business. It would also be an embarrassment for this correspondence to get into the wrong hands.

Third, in order of importance, is the information held on the payroll machine. This must be sustained so that the staff are paid correctly and on time. There is a legal requirement to protect much of this data under the Data Protection Act.

The point-of-sale machines only hold transient data. The data on these machines can be restored from the stock ledger machine up to the point of the last data interchange.

On the power supply front, should a power cut last for more than three hours or so, trading at the Dursley and Painswick branches would be severely impeded.

3.2   Specific Threats

The threats to the *Bookkeeper* system which should be countered are:

* loss of the main accounts ledger system data;
* unauthorised changes to the main accounts ledger system data;
* disclosure of data held on the word processing machine;
* loss or disclosure of staff records;
* loss of the machines through theft; and
* loss of power for extended periods of time.

3.3   Summary of Security Requirements

The main security requirements of the *Bookkeeper* system are:

* The computers should be kept physically secure so as to:
  - prevent unauthorised changes to the data on the various computers;
  - prevent unauthorised access to the various computers; and
  - prevent theft of the machines and their associated peripherals.

- Access to the rooms where the computers are installed should be restricted, as far as possible, to those people who need to have access to the computers.
- All vital data on all the machines should be backed up frequently and regularly so that no more than one day's transactions should be lost in the case of any disaster.
- Power supplies should be duplicated as far as possible so as to ensure that normal business can be conducted through a power cut lasting up to 12 hours.
- The physical protection for the computer rooms should be as if cash were kept in these rooms since ill-informed would-be burglars might try to trash the computer systems out of frustration.
- Cash should never be kept in any of the computer rooms.

4 System Security Policy

(This section describes the security features to be incorporated into the system so as to implement the requirements described above.)

4.1 Authentication

Authentication is the process of establishing the validity of the claimed identity. The general security principle is that access to cash and critical parts of the system should be restricted to those nominated by the management hence, before a person is allowed access to a facility, it is important that that person's identity is fully established before access is granted.

In a small business, such as J.R. Whitman Ltd., the number of employees (less than 30) is such that all authentication can be achieved by visual recognition. As the majority of transactions in the shops consist of cash transactions, there is virtually no requirement to establish the identity of a customer.

Visitors to the business, e.g., salesmen and service engineers, should be asked to verify their identity to a responsible member of staff before being escorted into the LSE. Normally, this identity validation will require the production of an identity card carrying a photograph of the subject.

There is minimal authentication in the ESE as all the systems are based on Microsoft Windows. The accounts ledger system at Dinklebury requires a password before a user can gain access to the system. In this business, the general principle is that if you have physical access to a computer then you have access to its facilities.

4.2 Access Control

The control of access to the various facilities of the business is fundamental to the security of J.R. Whitman Ltd.

4.2.1 Access Control in the GSE

There is absolutely no control of access by anyone in the GSE during normal business hours. Staff should attempt to keep customers under observation in the retail area so as to keep shoplifting down to an acceptable level.

4.2.2 Access Control in the LSE

LSE

Access to the LSE is restricted to the staff of J.R. Whitman Ltd. and accompanied visitors.

4.2.3   Access Control in the ESE

With the exception of the accounts ledger system, as indicated above, there are no access controls in the ESE.

4.3   Accounting

Accounting, in the information security sense, consists of the recording of the creation, transmission, modification or deletion of specific items of information specified in the security policy.

There is no formal accounting (in the information security sense) at J.R. Whitman Ltd. Accounting is essentially confined to the following:

- all retail transactions effected through the point-of-sale support system; and
- ensuring that all customers and visitors have left the premises at the end of trading hours each day.

4.4   Audit

Audit consists of monitoring events and the examination of audit trail to detect anomalies which may indicate breaches of the security policy.

Since J.R. Whitman Ltd. does not keep detailed records of information system transactions, there is virtually no formal information system audit policy.

5   Administration of Security

(This section specifies who is responsible for the various aspects of the security of the system and how it is to be administered and maintained.)

5.1   Management Roles and Responsibilities

The proprietor of J.R. Whitman Ltd., Mr James Whitman, is ultimately responsible for all security matters associated with the business.

Mr George Whitman, as general manager, is responsible for the implementation and administration of security within the business. In particular, he is responsible for:

- The security training and awareness of all J.R. Whitman staff.
- The drafting of detailed security orders for specific staff members, in particular, the managers of each of the three retail stores.
- The drawing up of staff duty rosters for the carrying out of various routine security tasks.
- In the event of a security incident, the carrying out of an enquiry whose purpose is to determine exactly what led up to the incident, what happened and what changes should be implemented to reduce the risk of such an incident being repeated.

PK Management Plc and Grunt Thornbush & Partners shall be called upon for specialist advice as needed.

5.2   Security Operating Procedures

5.2.1   Operations

5.2.2   Backups

Incremental backups shall be carried out daily. The point-of-sale machines shall exchange data with the stock ledger machine; the accounts ledger, the stock ledger and the word processing machines should be backed up onto Zip discs.

100% backups of the accounts ledger, the stock ledger and the word processing machines should be carried out fortnightly to DAT tape. There should be two copies of all backup tapes, one to be kept at Dinklebury and the second, fire copy, at Dursley.

5.3   Configuration Control

As far as possible, all bought-in software packages should be the latest. However, before any new software is brought into service on any of the operational computers, it should be thoroughly tested offline.

Appendix E

System Threats and Countermeasures

E.1 Introduction

In any straightforward information system, the threats can be divided into three groups:

- threats to the level of service;
- threats to the Information base; and
- threats leading to the leakage of sensitive information.

The overall spectrum of threats can be divided, rather crudely, into the 20 categories shown in Table E.1. A book such as this cannot prioritise these threat categories. This has to be carried out by the practitioner on the ground. It is the purpose of this appendix to help the practitioner to perform the necessary analysis so that a sensible and appropriate set of countermeasures can be chosen.

E.2 Threats to the Level of Service

Service levels can be affected partially or can be completely removed. Complete loss of service means that nobody is deriving any benefit from the information system. In most organisations, this can have serious and costly repercussions if this situation is allowed to persist for any length of time. Any countermeasures should minimise the likelihood of a complete loss of service or should ensure that some service is restored with the minimum of delay and that full service is restored as soon as possible.

A partial loss of service can manifest itself as either some degradation in performance or as the loss of some useful facilities. There are no particular

Table E.1: System threat prioritisation ckecklist

Threat	Ser	Priority					
		P1	P2	P3	P4	P5	P6
Power Loss	1						
Hardware Failure	2						
Software Crash	3						
Operator Error	4						
Malicious Inside Action	5						
Computer Virus	6						
Fire	7						
Explosion	8						
Floods	9						
Earthquakes	10						
Sabotage & Arson	11						
Disk Failure	12						
Data Corruption	13						
Inaccurate Data	14						
Unauthorised Access	15						
Hacking	16						
Media Leakage	17						
Theft of Media	18						
Tempest	19						
Communications	20						

countermeasures for partial losses as such except that when a partial loss does occur, checks should be made that it is not a symptom of an impending complete loss of service.

Complete loss of service can be be brought about in a number of ways:

Loss of power (electricity supply): this is quite serious. Unfortunately, the electricity supply companies do not guarantee a continuous supply of electricity to any customer. Computer systems are particularly vulnerable to very short breaks in supply (lasting only fractions of a second) which occur frequently during thunderstorms.

Breakdown of the computer equipment: although serious when such faults actually occur, computer breakdowns are becoming much rarer as the equipment is increasing in reliability. An individual computer system is liable to break down for some reason or another about once every year or so. The most likely component to fail, and cause the breakdown, is the power supply unit (PSU) followed by a terminal (visual display unit and keyboard).

Software malfunction: software errors which result in the computer system stopping dead in its tracks occur all too often especially after changes or upgrades to the software. Such occurrences are sufficiently common and notorious for a jargon term of "crash" to be created for them.

Operator error: humans have the unfortunate ability to make errors. With computer systems, some erroneous commands or sequences of commands can result in the computer system exhibiting the symptoms of a software malfunction.

Computer virus: if a computer system becomes infected with a computer virus (see Chapter 12), this may well result in complete or partial loss of service.

Environmental disaster: sometimes events such as earthquakes, floods, fires or explosions damage the equipment and its environment to such an extent that a service is no longer possible.

E.2.1 Power Supplies

The loss of power can result in rather more severe consequences than merely the loss of service from the information system for the duration of the power cut. Firstly, large database server computers usually take up to 20 minutes to initialise themselves before they are in a condition to offer any form of user service. Secondly, any transactions which were in the course of execution at the time of the power cut will have to be identified, undone and restarted. In extreme cases, the database can be in an inconsistent state as a direct result of the power cut; this will require possibly hours of work to reconstitute the database from a system dump and the transaction log file.

Fortunately, recent advances in technology have made the threat of a power cut relatively easy and cheap to deal with. A number of solutions are suggested below in decreasing order of cost.

1. If, as in some defence organisations, the threat is seen to be that the power loss will be as a result of deliberate enemy hostile action, then a comprehensive solution may be appropriate; dual independent feeds from the National Grid backed up by an emergency standby diesel generator. (The capacity of the generator must be such that it can supply the computer systems and the environmental conditioning equipment.)

2. Many commercial organisations with large computer centres are still worried by the threat of power cuts, but do not see these resulting from deliberate enemy action. Under these conditions a standby diesel generator is an alternative to dual independent feeds from the National Grid.

3. With the advance in computer technology it is now possible to service small- to medium-sized concerns using computer systems which consume less than 10kVA and do not require any environmental conditioning plant. For a sum of about $\frac{1}{5}$ of the cost of the computer equipment, it is possible to install an "intelligent" Uninterruptable Power Supply (UPS) which can sustain the power requirement of the computer system for a couple of hours or so. Various plant rooms containing communications equipment also require protection.

4. Individual workstations and personal computers can be protected from short power cuts (e.g. up to 10 minutes or so) by a simple UPS costing a few hundred dollars: $300 (£200) for a PC, $600 (£400) for a Unix graphics workstation.

As a general rule of thumb, is is usually cost-effective to install standby power arrangements for computer systems which are supplying a service to a number of users. (Such computer systems are usually called *servers*). However this cannot be said of individual workstations. Fortunately, PCs deal with power cuts very robustly; the same cannot be said for Unix workstations. Some consideration should be given as to whether a stand–alone workstation warrants an UPS. Unix workstations which are served from centralised file servers are not worth protecting.

There is one class of information systems for which this simple rule of thumb does not apply: the class of system which must supply a non–stop service, such as a safety critical nuclear reactor control system or an online operational military command and control system. In such cases, the manager must seek up-to-date specialist advice for the protection of power supplies.

E.2.2 Hardware Faults

Computer hardware faults can happen at any time. The effects of such faults can be minimised by a number of measures:

1. The use of special multi–processor equipment with multiple peripheral systems controlled by special systems software designed to provide graceful degradation in the presence of faults.
2. The use of "hot standby" equipment which is able to take over the role of the faulty equipment at a few moments notice.
3. The use of local "cold standby" equipment which can take over the role of the faulty equipment in a matter of an hour or so.
4. The use of some remote equipment earmarked to take over the role of the faulty equipment in a matter of a day or so.
5. The implementation of a maintenance call-out contract with an agency so that service is restored within an agreed period.
6. Casual maintenance.

These technologies range from the fairly pricey (a TANDEM system costs from two to three times its conventional equivalent) to the fairly cheap. Generally, the cost of a maintenance contract which will get an engineer on site within four hours of a call out will cost about 12–15% of the capital cost of the equipment per annum.

Having said that the more elaborate solutions are expensive to implement, the inappropriate use of the cheaper solutions can be even more expensive in the long run. In particular, the cost of the additional operators required to maintain the required level of service when using option 3 above more than outweighs any savings in the initial hardware costs within two years or so.

E.2.3 Software Crashes

Software faults arise in a number of circumstances:

- Newly installed bespoke software: it is impossible to test such software thoroughly before it is brought into service. The majority of the errors in the software arise from errors in the design of the software (i.e., the software was coded to perform incorrect actions) and the remaining errors consist of coding errors (i.e., the design was correct but there were errors in the software coding).
- Newly upgraded system software: the suppliers of system software go to great lengths to check and test features that have changed and features newly introduced into the software. However, it is impossible for these suppliers to know all the uses that users subject the system software to. There is a risk that when the underlying system software of an information system is upgraded, the behaviour of the information system will change and even may not work properly.
- Newly upgraded applications software: the same remarks as for system software apply; however, in general, the consequences are not quite so severe — the information system is normally constructed around several application programs; the failure of one program may not result in the sudden failure of the whole system.
- Software that has been patched: occasionally, software suppliers issue emergency amendments to their software in the form of binary patches which are applied directly to the programs by the customer. All too frequently, these patches cure the immediate problem but generate several others. Worse still, some users apply unauthorised patches to working software; this almost always results in trouble.

The countermeasures to these problems are straightforward and simple:

1. **Never** allow patched software to be used live in an operational information system.
2. **Always** trial upgraded software on a standby set of hardware to check for unexpected behaviour before such software is brought into operational service.
3. Where possible, retain the previous suite of software so that if the new software configuration exhibits signs of trouble, the system can revert to the previous working configuration.

E.2.4 Operator Errors

The term *operator* here refers to anyone who has terminal access to the system. In general, one can divide the world into four groups:

System operators: these are the people who run and administer the system.

Authorised users: these are the people who either make use of the system by supplying it with data or who derive benefit from the results generated by the system or both.

Programmers: these are the people who designed and coded the programs which comprise the system.

The rest of the world: comprises anyone who is not a system operator, an authorised user or a programmer.

Computer systems execute the commands typed in by the human operators. Software is rarely so robust that it can cope with any sequence of characters typed into it. Similarly, arbitrary sequences of apparently correct commands can confuse software to such an extent that it crashes. Occasionally an operator will deliberately type in commands which he or she knows will cause the system to crash; this may be out of malice or even for totally irrational reasons.

It is impossible to eliminate all operator errors. However, there are a number of measures which can be taken to reduce them to a reasonable minimum:

1. Operator training: make sure that all system operators and authorised users know and understand the correct procedures for the proper running of the system.
2. Ensure that all system operators and authorised users have been screened so as to establish that they are suitably trustworthy to have access to the system.
3. When programmers need access to the system they should always be escorted by a knowledgeable system operator to ensure that the programmers cannot perform any unauthorised transaction undetected.
4. Ensure that the rest of the world is not permitted to get physical access to any part of the system.

E.2.5 Computer Viruses

The effects of computer viruses manifest themselves in a variety of ways ranging from the irritating nuisance to the catastrophic collapse of the system. Once a system has been infected, the eradication of the virus can be a time-consuming and costly business. Reducing the risk of infection should be achieved using a policy based on the recommendations listed in Chapter 12. Part of the policy should be a procedure for decontaminating an infected system.

E.2.6 Environmental Disasters

Environmental disasters can take many forms. In almost every case, they are accompanied by a loss of power. The strategy for dealing with them is to arrange the system so that the effects of any such disasters on the system are minimised, and to arrange for service to be restored as soon as possible after the disaster. The main forms of such disasters are:

- **Fire**: this is an ever present hazard. The most likely causes of fire are:
  - faulty electrical wiring;
  - kitchens;
  - domestic accommodation;
  - laboratories;
  - inflammable detritus.

  The risk of fire to an information system is minimised by regular professional inspection and maintenance of all electrical wiring, general tidiness with regular collection of rubbish, and the siting of the computer centre as far away as possible from other hazardous accommodation.
- **Explosions**: these are normally associated with leaking inflammable gases or volatile liquids. Reducing the risk of explosions to an information system is, again, a matter of siting and careful inspection and maintenance.
- **Floods**: these arise from three main possible causes:
  - badly maintained fabric of the building (which is no longer weatherproof);
  - burst water pipes or water resulting from fire fighting elsewhere in the building;
  - rising rivers or lakes overflowing into buildings.

  The risk of flood damage to an information system is reduced by suitable siting of the computer centre — not in a basement where flood water tends to collect — and the regular inspection and maintenance of the fabric of the building.
- **Earthquakes**: these are a hazard in California, Japan and a number of other Far Eastern countries, and countries around the Eastern Mediterranean. In those areas, professional advice is available for the siting and construction of buildings so that the effects of most earthquakes can be minimised. Because earthquakes are frequently accompanied by fire and explosions, other precautions listed above are also applicable.
- **Sabotage and arson**: the saboteur will have to get to the computer centre building to initiate the deed. The principal defenses are the restriction of access to the site to those who have a need, the screening of all such people and, where possible, the siting of the building well away from public access and vehicle parking areas.

There are a number of possible measures that can be taken to minimise the effects of environmental disasters on information systems:

1. careful siting of the important components of the information system;
2. good physical and personnel security;
3. regular inspection and maintenance of the buildings and plant;
4. good housekeeping including the timely disposal of flammable waste.

E.3 Threats to the Information Base

There are five main threats to the integrity of the data held by the system:

- failure of the storage devices holding the information;
- software malfunction which corrupts all or part of the data held by the system;
- users inserting incorrect information;
- unauthorised personnel gaining access to the system with sufficient privileges to make changes to the data;
- viruses (See the previous section).

Modern discs are very reliable; however, they can still fail. Whatever storage technology is used, there should be a data integrity policy which prescribes the frequency and manner of data backups. If backing store failure is deemed to be a particular concern, the use of RAID technology can help in stretching the time between storage system failures to in excess of 10 years or so. The full cost of this technology is about five times that of unprotected discs.

Even if disc storage becomes 100% reliable, there is still a need for data backups as now the most common cause of the loss or corruption of data is a combination of operator error and the malfunctioning of software.

E.4 Threats Leading to Information Leakage

Information can leak out of an information system via one of the following routes:

- unauthorised personnel gaining access to the system;
- careless handling of discs and magnetic tapes holding copies of the data of the information system;
- TEMPEST;
- hacking;
- tapping into the communications.

E.5 Choice of Countermeasures

For any threat, there is a spectrum of countermeasures. The problem is the determination of which countermeasure(s) is (are) appropriate in the circumstances. Within each group of countermeasures, some will be more convenient and less expensive than others to implement. Unfortunately, the less costly measures are frequently less effective in preventing problems from occurring. To simplify the choice of countermeasure, each will be classified within its functional group. To simplify this process, each countermeasure will be assigned an effectiveness value in the range F1–F6 — where a measure classified as F6 is thought to be more effective than one classified as F1.

Table E.2: Countermeasure prioritisation checklist

Functional Area	Ser	F6	F5	F4	F3	F2	F1
Backup Power Supplies	1						
Communications Configuration	2						
Communications Cryptography	3						
Communications Protocols	4						
Data Backup	5						
Documentation	6						
Fall Back Configuration	7						
Media Handling	8						
Operator Training	9						
Password Policy	10						
Personnel Security	11						
Physical Security	12						
Plant Inspection & Maintenance	13						
Programming Language & Development	14						
Redundant Disk Technology	15						
Siting & Layout	16						
S/W Upgrade Test System	17						
System Architecture	18						
System Configuration Control	19						
System Design, Development & Installation	20						
System Delivery & Installation	21						
System Specification	22						
Tempest	23						
Virus Procedures	24						

Backup Power Supplies

1. A simple UPS.
2. An intelligent UPS with extended gap capacity.

3. A combination of an UPS and standby generator (the UPS is needed to cover the gap while the generator is running up to speed).
4. Dual independent feeds from the National Grid.
5. Dual independent feeds from the National Grid and a standby generator.

Communications Configuration
Communications Cryptography
Communications Protocols
Data Backup
1. Simple weekly disc backups.
2. Dual weekly backups, one held in a remote fire store.
3. Dual weekly backups with daily incremental dumps.

Documentation
Fall Back Software Configuration
Media Handling
Operator Training
Password Policy
Personal Security
Physical Security
Plant Inspection & Maintenance
Programming Language & Development Environment
Redundant Disk Technology
Siting & Layout
Software Upgrade Test System
System Architecture
System Configuration Control
System Design, Implementation & Development
System Delivery & Installation
System Specification
Tempest
1. Site equipment at least 25m from car parks and perimeter fence.
2. Use of equipment complying with Part 15 of FCC rules.
3. Use of equipment complying with Part 15 of FCC rules. with filtered power supplies and only local terminals
4. Use of UK regulation compliant equipment.

Virus Procedures

E.6 Summary

There are a wide variety of possible threats to an information system. The more important of these are categorised in Table E.1. This table should be used as a checklist to assess and prioritise the various threat categories. To counter these threats there are some 25 types of countermeasure available to the manager. These are summarised in Table E.2. The nature of the specific threats should determine which types of measure should be used and to what degree.

Appendix F

Example List of Security Countermeasures

This list is an adaption of that compiled by Captain Sean Hoag for use in his MSc dissertation. This, in turn, was derived, in the main, from the Canadian Forces Analysis Methodology.

This list is composed of more than 70 safeguards For convenience, they are grouped. This list is not comprehensive by any means; it is intended as a guide to the range of available defensive measures. Again, it must be stressed (as it is elsewhere in this book) that a particular security policy will be composed of a *subset* of these measures plus some others not mentioned here. The greatest danger that the author foresees with this list, is that the number of these measures referenced in a security plan becomes a measure of the quality of that security plan.

F.1 Access Control

F.1.1 Communications

1. **Network separation.** The creation and maintenance of separate networks for different classes of users. This is only appropriate where there is the minimum of overlapping of areas of interest between the various user groups on the different networks.
2. **Mandatory access control.** This requires the assignment of sensitivity labels to the communication resources. Further, it requires a trusted and suitably trained manager to assign semantics to the labels and labels to both subjects and objects.
3. **Discretionary access control.** This consists of controlling access to network resources by use of conventional file permission bits.

F.1.2 Covert Channel Control

1. **Clear all users to highest level.** This is tantamount to the implementation of a dedicated system.
2. **Constrain system functionality.** An example of a limitation which reduces the effectiveness of some implementations of covert channels is to prevent user processes from dynamically changeing their priority.
3. **Use an operating system** which delivers a guaranteed level of service to specific applications (e.g., the Cambridge University *Nemesis*[1] Operating System).
4. **Configuration control.** The exploitation of covert channels requires the cooperation of a user process at a high level of sensitivity with a process running at a lower level of sensitivity. The system should be configured so as to minimise the opportunities for exploiting covert channels: e.g., by maintaining close control over the access privileges to shared resources and limiting the software available on the system.
5. **Audit.** If covert channels cannot be eliminated, then specific audit mechanisms should be introduced so as to monitor the possible covert channels and minimise the potential for their exploitation.

F.1.3 Discretionary Access Control

1. **Ensure all users have need-to-know privileges.**
2. **Use an operating system certified to functionality FC2:** for example, Unix or Windows NT4.0 with basic security enhancements — which ensures that the systems are configured securely rather than the default out-of-the-box configuration (see Appendix A).

F.1.4 Mandatory Access Control

1. **Clear all users to highest level.** If all users are cleared to to the highest level of sensitivity of information processed within the system, then the need for a Mandatory Access Control enforcement regime is eliminated.
2. **Use an operating system certified to at least functionality FB2:** e.g., "secure" versions of Unix and Windows NT4.0.
3. **Time domain control:** run separate sessions at different times for each sensitivity level. This is not very convenient, but may be the only practical method.

---

[1] Designed by Paul Barham, Richard Black, Robin Fairbairns, Eoin Hyden, Ian Leslie, Derek McAuley and Timothy Roscoe

F.1.5 Physical Access Control

Enclose the system inside a secure perimeter with controlled access points so
that only those entitled to enter are permitted to do so. A record should be
kept of those entering and leaving the controlled area so it is known who is
in the controlled area at any given time.

F.2 Accountability

F.2.1 Transactions

1. **Authentication.** Authentication is defined as the process of establishing
   the validity of a claimed identity. This is required so that the system can
   administer the access controls appropriate to the user.
2. **Non–repudiation.** The use of digital signatures and trusted intermediaries can be used to ensure that an entity cannot revoke a transaction.
3. **Separation of duties.** Having two (or more) people required to perform critical system functions may be an acceptable way to account for
   critical transactions. Strong procedures and/or technical mechanisms are
   required to enforce the separation of duties.

F.2.2 Configuration

1. **Software signatures.** Software has embedded within it a digital signature which is verified before execution.
2. **Hardware signatures.** Individual processors can have unique digital
   signatures embedded within them. These signatures are verified before
   the hardware is brought into operational mode. This is over and above
   the requirement in any certified system that the software should validate
   the correct functioning of the hardware required to defend the Trusted
   Computer Base before the system is put into operational mode.
3. **Tamper resistant construction.** Hardware can be constructed to resist attempts to tamper with it.
4. **Tamper evident construction.** Hardware can be constructed so that
   attempts to tamper with it can be readily detected.
5. **Limit the transfer of executable objects.** It is possible to constrain
   the system in such a way that certain functions may be executed on
   specified CPUs.

F.3 Accuracy

F.3.1 Communications

1. **Digital signatures.** Digital signatures may be used to identify the originator and prevent the undetected modification of a communication.
2. **Integrity check value:** an end–to–end Transmission level protocol data unit sum check; this is the default for some protocols.
3. **Trusted communications channels** composed of dedicated physical circuits and other communications resources managed in such a way which guaratees separation from other circuits.
4. In some cases, one can resort to such exotic techniques as **spread spectrum transmission** and **forward error correcting codes.**

F.3.2 Storage

1. **RAID techniques** which provide data redundancy using techniques such as duplication and striped error correcting techniques (RAID1 and RAID5).
2. **Integrity check value:** an entity level data unit sum check; this is the default for most storage devices and database systems.
3. **Error correcting codes:** see RAID techniques above.
4. **Journals.** Database and File System journals keep a copy of all transactions conducted on the system so that recovery can be performed from the last checkpoint. This mechanism should protect the system from both hardware failures and most erroneous transactions.
5. **Checkpointing.** Database and file system checkpointing keeps a copy of the database or the file system so that, in the event of a failure, the system can be rolled back to a known state.

F.4 Availability

F.4.1 Communications

1. **Dedicated communications system:** a communication system which is both physically and logically separated from all other communication systems.
2. **Redundant communications systems:** provide a backup communication system to handle a breakdown in the primary communication system. This backup system can be shared with other communication requirements.
3. **Redundancy within a communications system:** where there are spare communication resources (e.g., circuits and switches) which can be

used to bypass breakdowns and congestion within the communications system.

4. **Media diversity** is where redundancy is provided by providing a choice of transmission media, for example: telephone and citizen band radio.

5. **Path diversity** is essentially providing alternative circuits between the sender and the receiver (see **redundancy within a communications system** above).

6. **Precedence and preemption** consists of prioritisation of communication users and uses, and allowing higher priority traffic to obtain access to communications systems ahead of lower priority traffic.

7. **Dynamic reconfiguration** is a normal feature of tactical military communication systems in which at any one time a proportion of the communication resources is detached from the communications system while it is relocated. For such a system to work successfully, the network nodes must be capable of handling the loss of circuits to other nodes, and the gaining of new circuits, with little or no warning.

8. **Graceful degradation** is the ability of a communications system to continue to provide a useable service after the unexpected loss of some communication resources.

9. **Training** of relevant personnel in the efficient running of the communication system and the efficient handling of system crises.

F.4.2 Logical Denial

1. **User training** to make efficient (frugal) use of system resources.

2. **Reduced user functionality** as a method of reducing the load on the system.

3. **Reduced number of users** as an alternative method of reducing the load on the system.

F.4.3 Personnel

1. **Cross training of personnel** is adding to the skills of an individual so as to ensure that service is maintained during the unplanned absence of key personnel.

2. **Deployment of trained personnel** is using the experience of some senior personnel to cover for the absence of skilled personnel. An extreme example of this is the deployment of management personnel to carry out operative tasks to sustain a level of service through a strike situation.

3. **Shift scheduling** is a technique of providing cover during a (short term) shortage of trained personnel.

F.4.4 Physical Denial

1. **Standby redundant sites:** the provision of alternative resources at physically separate locations to cater for such disasters as flood and fire. This is a common and prudent precaution undertaken by many businesses. Firm "A" will make mutual arrangements with firm "B" such that if one firm's resources become unavailable, the other firm will host the vital processing of the stricken firm until such time as the stricken firm can replace the missing resources.
2. **Standby redundant equipment:** to provide fast replacement resources in the event of equipment failure. Standby computers and standby generators are used by some businesses.
3. **On-site spares:** held for the rapid replacement of certain components and consumables to minimise breaks in service when certain components fail or become exhausted.
4. **Site hardening:** is taking precautions so as to minimise the effects of such natural disasters as floods and earthquakes.
5. **Training:** of personnel in the efficient handling of system crises.

F.4.5 Environmental Damage

It is essential to draw up contingency plans to deal with a range of natural and man-made disasters:

1. **fire**;
2. **flood**;
3. **lightning** and, in some parts of the world;
4. **earthquake**.

F.5 Data Exchange

F.5.1 Communications Security

1. **Encryption** to confine the contents of messages to those entitled to read them.
2. **Trusted communications channels** composed of dedicated physical circuits and other communications resources managed in a way which guarantees separation from other circuits.

F.5.2 Covert Channel.

1. **Link level encryption.** The use of link level encryption removes some covert channel mechanisms.

2. **Covert channel elimination.** For example, by using a low functionality dialect of X25.

3. **Object reuse control.** The uncontrolled reuse of information system resources is the main cause of covert storage channels. The resources requiring particular care are:
   - disk blocks and file system buffers;
   - magnetic tapes and cartridges;
   - floppy disks;
   - cpu caches, registers and video buffers.

F.5.3 Radiation Security

To reduce the leakage of information through spurious electromagnetic radiation:

1. **Fibre optics**: where possible, signals should be carried in fibre optic cables rather than copper cables. Correctly shielded and terminated copper cable does not radiate much but fibre optic cable radiates less. Once an installation starts to age, the effectiveness of the shielding of copper cabling will diminish, thus increasing the risks of unwanted electromagnetic radiation.

2. The correct use of **siting, zoning and layout** of wiring, metal trunking and metal pipework in a sensitive area can reduce the risks of unwanted electromagnetic radiation to an acceptable level.

3. **Screened rooms** are a last resort reserved for the most extreme circumstances where the most sensitive information has to be processed in difficult conditions. They are expensive to build and maintain and are awkward to use.

F.5.4 Transmission Security

These are techniques normally associated with military communications in an active electronic warfare environment:

1. **Low probability of intercept techniques,**
2. **Spread spectrum;**
3. **Frequency hopping;**
4. **Null steerable antennae;** and
5. **Burst transmission.**

F.5.5 Traffic Flow Security

More techniques normally associated with military communications in an active electronic warfare environment:

1. **Link level crypto with fill** so as to diguise the true packet length and the quantity of information actually being transfered.
2. **Generation of dummy connections and traffic** so as to confuse an eavesdropper.
3. **Trusted communications channels** composed of dedicated physical circuits and other communications resources managed in such a way which guarantees separation from other circuits so as to minimise the risk of interception (eavesdropping).

F.6 Authentication

Mechanisms to establish the identitity of people before they are allowed access to the system:

1. **physical access control** with active checking of the identity of an individual attempting to gain entry;
2. **passwords**;
3. **tokens**, for example, a magnetic card system;
4. **biometric access control devices** such as palm print readers and eye iris readers; and
5. **digital signatures** normally used as an authentication mechanism for electronic access.

None of these authentication systems are perfect. However, biometric devices seem to have a lot of promise once some of the basic practical problems have been solved and the devices get less expensive.

F.7 Audit

Auditing up to now has been a "Cinderella" area. The problem is the quantity of audit records that a computer system can generate. The dilemma is whether to record every event and be swamped by the quantity of data, or to record the barest minimum and run the risk of completely missing a significant event. Some automatic assistance for the auditor is of considerable help. The question then becomes how much automated assistance should be given to the auditor. Here are some examples:

1. **Audit with human monitoring** in which there is the very minimum of automation; all possible significant events are presented to the human monitor who has to determine what action should be taken, if any. In such a system, the human monitor can operate at full efficiency only for short periods at a time before making mistakes from boredom or fatigue. This type of system is only useful in circumstances where there is a shift

of at least two monitors who have other duties and can take turns at the monitoring task. A lot of behavioural information about such systems was gained from the early automated air space monitoring systems during the cold war.

2. **Audit with automated alarms** is the next stage of automation. The audit system is allowed to make a decision as to when a significant event may have occured and then draws the event to the attention of a monitor who has to make a final decision as to what action (if any) should be taken as a result of the system raising an alarm. Such a system should be practical to implement and has the advantage that the human monitor can be tasked with other security duties between alarms.

3. **Audit with automated corrective action** is almost full automation of the audit task. A reliable system with minimal false alarms is still beyond the state-of-the-art at the turn of the millennium.

F.8 Personnel

The screening of all personnel who have access to the information system is perhaps the most important single aspect of risk management. In Chapter 4, five distinct levels of personnel trustworthiness were defined. The degree of access accorded to any individual should be limited to their degree of trustworthiness. The corollary of this is that personnel concerned with the system administration should be cleared to a level commensurate with the highest level of sensitivity of information held in the system.

Secondly, system users should be restricted in their access to information held by the system in accordance with their degree of trustworthiness.

Appendix G

Glossary of Information Security Terms

Access Control List (ACL): associated with an *object* (usually a file or a device such as a terminal or a printer) and specifies a list of subjects (normally users) and their individual access rights with respect to the object.

Active–X: a Microsoft proprietary facility which provides for multi–media functionality to be embedded into documents suitable for transfer across the Internet.

Audit: an independent review and examination of the system records and activities to determine the effectiveness of the system security measures and the degree of conformance with the agreed system security policy. (It may well be part of the security policy that trusted system software is used to generate some of these records.)

Audit trail: a set of system records from which the history of events can be reconstructed as part of an investigation.

Authentication: the verification of a claimed identity.

Authorisation: the determination of which system resources a user may use.

Availability: the term which describes that proportion of the time that a system is available to the end user. Non-availability is the time when the system is not available to the user, either because it is not working at all or the system management have exclusive use of the system for maintenance.

Bastion: *see* Firewall.

Bell and LaPadula Security Model: a formal specification of the most common governmental security policy. It can be summarised as follows:

- No *subject* (person or device) may access an *object* (information) the sensitivity of which is greater than the clearance of the subject.

- (Known as the *–property*) no subject may write to an object whose sensitivity is less than the clearance of the subject.

Boot Sector Infector (BSI): a form of virus which replaces the boot code with itself and places the boot code on another part of the disc. Such a virus is activated by booting from the infected disc. The virus installs itself in RAM as a *Terminate and Stay Resident* (TSR) Program.

BSI: *see* Boot Sector Infector.

CERT (Computer Emergency Response Team): is a security information coordination centre. The original was set up at the Software Engineering Institute, Carnegie Mellon University (Pittsburg, PA) as a direct result of the 1988 Internet Worm incident. Since then, other nations have set up their own CERTs which may have different official titles but are often referred to as CERTs.

CESG: the abbreviation for the Communications Electronics Security Group which is the UK national technical authority for information security matters.

Checksum: the result of performing an arithmetic computation on a block of data, such as a file or packet. The integrity of the data may be checked at some later time by performing an identical computation on the data and comparing the results with the original.

Companion virus: a form of virus that exploits the search sequence of the MS–DOS `COMMAND.COM` program. Because ".COM" programs take precedence over ".EXE" and ".BAT" programs, it is possible for a program "xx.COM" to take control over a "xx.EXE" or a "xx.BAT" program in the same directory. The innocent user invokes the virus by the command "xx"; the "xx.COM" program executes and when it has done it may pass control to the "xx.EXE" (or "xx.BAT") program. The virus attempts to propagate itself by making a copy of itself and changing its name to "yy.COM" in a directory containing a file "yy.EXE" or "yy.BAT".

Compartmented security mode: a mode of computer operation in which all the users are cleared to access the most sensitive information held by the system but are only given access to part of the data using mandatory access controls to restrict the data any particular user may access.

Confinement: the prevention of the flow of data from one domain to another.

Covert channel: a mechanism, other than the normal programming mechanisms, which permits the flow of information. Usually covert channels are either timing channels or storage channels. The threat is that, because covert channels are difficult to monitor and suppress, they may be used to subvert the security policy enforcement mechanisms.

Cracker: more usually called a "hacker": a person who derives gain or satisfaction from attempting (and frequently succeeding) to gain unauthorised access to computer systems.

Daemon: the basic real time service provider in a Unix system. It is the Unix equivalent of a DOS/Windows TSR program.

Dedicated security mode: a mode of running a computer system which makes no attempt to use computer hardware or software to enforce a security policy.

Denial of service: the prevention of a legitimate user obtaining the expected benefits from an information system. This can arise from accidental or malicious causes.

DES (Data Encryption Standard): the first supplier independent standard mechanism for the encryption of data which allowed users to pass encrypted data to each other. It was formally adopted by the US National Bureau of Standards in November 1976. It is a development of IBM's "Lucifer" cipher system. A modified form of the DES algorithm is used to encrypt Unix passwords. Modern (late 1990s) hardware is sufficiently powerful as to render the DES algorithm obsolescent: it is theoretically possible to procure computers and specialised hardware which could perform a brute force crack of a DES encoded message in less than 12 hours.

Discretionary access control: access permissions and denials set up by someone other than a user acting in the role of the System Security Officer.

Electronic Security Environment (ESE): the electronic domain which contains all the data held in electronic form together with the electronic systems which manipulate the data.

File infector: a form of virus which appends its code to an MS–DOS executable program. Such a virus arranges to be executed before the host program when the host program is invoked. The virus will attempt to infect other executable files normally using the PATH system variable as a guide. When it has completed its execution it will return control to the host program.

Firewall computer: a computer system put between an external network (such as the Internet) and a computer or private network so as to minimise the risk of an external Cracker (*qv*) gaining access to the private system.

FTP (File Transfer Protocol): is the protocol used in conjunction with TCP/IP to transfer files across the Internet. The program normally used to perform this service is usually called ftp.

Global Security Environment (GSE): the general security environment in which the system is located. It covers everything outside the control of the system manager up to the establishment perimeter fence and possibly a short way beyond.

Hacker: *see* Cracker.

Java: a portable (usually interpreted) programming language originally designed to provide additional functionality for Internet browsers.

Kerberos: a network authentication system developed as part of the MIT Athena Project. It is a "third party" authentication service, trusted by other network services, to prove a user's identity to the other hosts and services in the network. Kerberos was designed specifically to counter "spoof" and "playback" attacks on the network.

Label: for the purposes of information security, a machine readable marking associated with an *object* (usually a file, record, field or document) defining the sensitivity and/or the codeword of the *object*.

Local Security Environment (LSE): that part of the security domain under the control of the System Manager. Normally, it should include all the rooms containing any equipment associated with the system.

Logic Bomb: *see* Sleeper.

MALPAS: a suite of static analysis programs designed and written by RSRE (now DERA (Malvern)).

Mandatory access control: the control of access by subjects to objects in accordance with national security policy. More specifically, this usually consists of restricting the access to sensitive data to those people who have been cleared to that level of sensitivity, or higher. (*See also* Bell and LaPadula Security model).

Multi–level security mode: a mode of computer system operation in which there is data at a number of sensitivity levels and which handles users, not all of whom have been cleared to access the highest level of sensitivity. The system is relied upon to enforce the national security rules (*see* Mandatory Access Controls).

NSA: the US National Security Agency which is ultimately responsible for the approval of technical security policies for US federal agencies. Its main activities are signals intelligence (SIGINT) and information systems security (INFOSEC).

Object: a passive entity containing or able to receive data. Normally an object is a disc, tape, file, record, field or document.

Orange Book: the nickname for the book "Trusted Computer System Evaluation Criteria" published by the US DoD[26].

Packet: the name given to a data fragment which is a part of a message in a communications network. The sending station chops messages into packets to be transmitted to the receiving station. The receiving station collects all the packets of the original message so as to reconstitute it before finally delivering it to the addressee.

Password: a sequence of characters known only by the user and the system used to authenticate the user to the system (i.e., to convince the system that the user actually is who he says he is).

Privilege: a "permission" or other ability to carry out an operation on an object.

Risk: defined as the likelihood of a successful attack on a system.

Role: a user's set of responsibilities and privileges.

Sector: the smallest directly addressable unit of storage on a disc.

Sensitivity: the sensitivity of a piece of information is a measure of the cost associated with the disclosure of the information. Sensitivity is a synonym for security classification.

Sleeper: a covert section of program which lies dormant until it is activated by a *trigger*. When activated, a sleeper will execute code which may suppress software security features or carry out some action usually to the detriment of the rightful owner of the software and to the benefit of a third party.

Side effect: is any phenomenon which results incidentally from a system state change. This term is loosely associated with the undocumented phenomena arising from a state change or some phenomena which cannot be formally specified or tested for.

SPADE: a suite of static analysis programs designed and implemented by a team at Southampton University under Dr Bernard Carré.

Storage channel: a covert channel in which information can flow via storage locations which have not been flushed when the use of the storage locations is changed. An example of a storage channel is when a user deletes a file and then the system reallocates the sectors, previously used by the deleted file, to a new file without previously overwriting the original contents of the blocks.

Static analysis: a program testing technique which aims to detect programming anomalies (possible errors) from the analysis of the source code rather than attempting to execute the software. The first stage of static analysis is *control flow analysis* which attempts to determine all the possible paths through the program under analysis. The second stage of analysis is *data flow analysis* which determines which variables are actually used in the execution of the program. The third stage of analysis is *information flow analysis* which determines which inputs contribute to the outputs of the program under analysis. The final stage of analysis is *semantic analysis* which attempts to generate complete formulae for selected program outputs. The analysis tool set may also include a *partial program generator* which extracts the relevant parts of a program for a more detailed study.

System high security mode: a mode of running a computer system which makes use of computer hardware and software to implement a discretionary access control policy but does not use such technology to implement a mandatory access control policy. All users must be cleared to the level appropriate for the most sensitive information held by the system.

TEMPEST: a code word for the unintended radiation of information from electronic equipment.

Threat: an action or event which could prejudice the security of a system.

Timing channel: a form of covert channel in which information flows through the use and freeing of a system resource which can be observed by another process. It is possible, theoretically, for the process using and freeing the system resource to pass information, albeit at a very low rate, to any process able to observe the behaviour of the resource.

Trojan Horse: a computer program that purports to perform a useful service for the user while, at the same time, performs actions which may eventually subvert the security of the system, e.g., by making unauthorised copies of passwords.

Trusted Computer Base (TCB): the security protection mechanisms and the data structures which control their behaviour, which are responsible for the enforcement of the system security policy.

Trusted function: a system module whose correct operation is relied upon for the implementation of an aspect of the system security policy.

TSR program: a form of program than installs itself in an MS–DOS environment and then returns control to MS-DOS. Part of the installation process will consist of replacing an interrupt vector address with its own start address.

Virus: a program fragment, which may have a deleterious effect on a computer system, which has the capacity to replicate itself in such a way that it can infect other similar machines. (*See also* Boot Sector Infector, Companion virus, File infector *and* Worm.)

Vulnerability: the likelihood of a successful attack being mounted on a system.

Worm: a virus like program system that uses the communications network to propagate itself. The most famous example of a worm is the "Internet Worm" (*see* [6],[7] *and* [37]).

Appendix H

References & Bibliography

1. Bell, D.E. and LaPadula, L.J. "Secure Computer Systems: Unified Exposition and Multics Interpretation" Report MTR-2997 Rev1, MITRE Corporation, Bedford, Mass, 1976.
2. Bellovin, S.M. "Security Problems with the TCP/IP Protocol Suite", ACM Computer Communications Review, April 1989.
3. Brewer, D.F.C. and Nash, M.J. "The Chinese Wall Security Policy". Proceedings of the IEEE Symposium on Security and Privacy, Oakland, Ca, pp 206-214, May 1989.
4. Clark, D.D. and Wilson, D.R. "A Comparison of Commercial and Military Computer Security Policies". Proceedings of the IEEE Symposium on Security and Privacy, Oakland, Ca, pp 184-194, April 1987.
5. Cornwall, Hugo and Gold, Steve. "New Hacker's Handbook" (4th Edn), Century Hutchinson, 1989.
6. Denning, Peter J. "Computers Under Attack – Intruders, Worms and Viruses", Addison–Wesley, 1990.
7. Eichin, Mark W., and Rochlis, Jon A. "With Microscope and Tweezers: An Analysis of the Internet Virus of November 1988." Massachusetts Institute of Technology. February 1989.
8. Eizenburg G. "Mandatory Policy: A Secure Systems Model" ONERA/ CERT/DERI, Toulouse, France (undated).
9. Elmer-DeWitt, Philip. "The Kid Put Us Out of Action." Time, 132 (20): 76, November 14, 1988.
10. Forum on Risks to the Public in Computers and Related Systems. ACM Committee on Computers and Public Policy, Peter G. Neumann, Moderator. Internet mailing list. Issue 5.73, December 13, 1987.
11. Forum on Risks to the Public in Computers and Related Systems. ACM Committee on Computers and Public Policy, Peter G. Neumann, Moderator. Internet mailing list. Issue 7.85, December 1, 1988.

12. Forum on Risks to the Public in Computers and Related Systems. ACM Committee on Computers and Public Policy, Peter G. Neumann, Moderator. Internet mailing list. Issue 8.2, January 4, 1989.

13. Forum on Risks to the Public in Computers and Related Systems. ACM Committee on Computers and Public Policy, Peter G. Neumann, Moderator. Internet mailing list. Issue 8.9, January 17, 1989.

14. Forum on Risks to the Public in Computers and Related Systems. ACM Committee on Computers and Public Policy, Peter G. Neumann, Moderator. Internet mailing list. Issue 9.69, February 20, 1990.

15. Garfinkel S. L. "Pretty Good Privacy" O'Reilly & Associates, Inc. 1995.

16. Garfinkel S. L., and Spafford E. H. "Practical Unix Security" O'Reilly & Associates, Inc. 1991.

17. Goncalves M. "Firewalls Complete" McGraw–Hill, 1998.

18. Grammp, F. T., and Morris, R. H. "UNIX Operating System Security." AT&T Bell Laboratories Technical Journal, 63 (8): 1649-1672, October 1984.

19. Hinden, R., J. Haverty, and Sheltzer, A. "The DARPA Internet: Interconnecting Heterogeneous Computer Networks with Gateways." IEEE Computer Magazine, 16(9): 33-48, September 1983.

20. "Information Technology Security Evaluation Criteria (ITSEC)", ECSC–EEC–EAEC, Brussels, 1991.

21. JSP440 "The *(UK)* Defence Manual of Security", Vol 3 — Information Technology, MoD, April !995.

22. Landwehr, C.E., Heitmeyer, C.L. and McLean, J. "A Security Model for Military Message Systems" ACM Transactions on Computer Systems, Vol 2 No 3, pp 198-222, August 1984.

23. McLellan, Vin. "NASA Hackers: There's More to the Story." Digital Review, November 23, 1987, p. 80.

24. Morris, Robert, and Thompson, Ken. "Password Security: A Case History." Communications of the ACM, 22(11): 594-597, November 1979. Reprinted in UNIX System Manager's Manual, 4.3 Berkeley Software Distribution. University of California, Berkeley. April 1986.

25. Morris, Robert T. "A Weakness in the 4.2BSD Unix TCP/IP Software", AT&T Bell Labs Computer Science Technical Report 117, Feb 1985.

26. National Computer Security Center. Department of Defense Trusted Computer System Evaluation Criteria, Department of Defense Standard DOD 5200.28-STD, December, 1985.

27. Nemeth, Evi, Snyder, Garth and Seebass, Scott. "UNIX System Administration Handbook", Prentice Hall, 1989.

28. Quarterman, J. S., and Hoskins, J. C. "Notable Computer Networks." Communications of the ACM, 29 (10): 932-971, October 1986.

29. Reeds, J. A., and Weinberger, P. J. "File Security and the UNIX System Crypt Command." AT&T Bell Laboratories Technical Journal, 63 (8): 1673-1683, October 1984.

30. Ritchie, Dennis M. "On the Security of UNIX." May 1975. Reprinted in UNIX System Manager's Manual, 4.3 Berkeley Software Distribution. University of California, Berkeley. April 1986.

31. Russel, Deborah and Gangemi, G.T. "Computer Security Basics", O'Reilly & Associates, 1991.

32. Sams, Net "Maximum Internet Security: A Hacker's Guide", SAMS, July 1997

33. Schneier, Bruce. "Applied Cryptography", John Wiley & Sons Inc, 1996.

34. Schuman, Evan. "Bid to Unhook Worm." UNIX Today!, February 5, 1990, p. 1.

35. Seeley, Donn. "A Tour of the Worm". Department of Computer Science, University of Utah. December 1988.

36. Slade, Robert "Guide to Computer Viruses" Springer–Verlag 1994.

37. Spafford, E. H. The Internet Worm Program: An Analysis. Technical Report CSD-TR-823. Department of Computer Science, Purdue University. November 1988.

38. Steele, Guy L. Jr., Woods, Donald R., Finkel, Raphael A., Crispin, Mark R., Stallman, Richard M., and Goodfellow, Geoffrey S. The Hacker's Dictionary. New York: Harper and Row, 1988.

39. Stein, Jennifer G., Neuman, Clifford and Schiller, Jeffrey L. "Kerberos: An Authentication Service for Open Network Systems." USENIX Conference Proceedings, Dallas, Texas, Winter 1988, pp. 203-211.

40. Stoll, Clifford. "Stalking the Wily Hacker." Communications of the ACM, 31 (5): 484-497, May 1988.

41. Stoll, Clifford. The Cuckoo's Egg. New York: Doubleday, 1989.

42. Sun Microsystems. SunOS Reference Manual, Part Number 800-1751-10, May 1988.

43. Sun Microsystems. System and Network Administration, Part Number 800-1733-10, May 1988.

44. Sun Microsystems. Security Features Guide, Part Number 800-1735-10, May 1988.

45. Sun Microsystems. "Network File System: Version 2 Protocol Specification". Network Programming, Part Number 800-1779-10, May 1988, pp. 165-185.

46. Wack, John P. and Carnahan, Lisa J. "Computer Viruses and Related Threats: A Managememt Guide", National Institute of Standards and Technology Special Publication 500–166 (US Government Printing Office Document No 003–003–02955–6).

47. Wilson, Brian. "Systems: Concepts, Methodologies, and Applications" (2nd Ed). Wiley 1990.

48. Ziegler, Robert L. "Linux Firewalls", New Riders Publishing Nov 1999.

Index

225